Best Garden Plants *for* Minnesota *and* Wisconsin

Don Engebretson & Don Williamson

LONE PINE

Lone Pine Publishing International

Distributed by Lone Pine Publishing
1808 B Street NW, Suite 140
Auburn, WA, USA 98001
Website: www.lonepinepublishing.com

Library and Archives Canada Cataloguing in Publication
Engebretson, Don, 1955-
    Best garden plants for Minnesota and Wisconsin / Don Engebretson & Don Williamson.

Includes index.

ISBN-13: 978-1-55105-500-8
ISBN-10: 1-55105-500-7

1. Plants, Ornamental--Minnesota. 2. Plants, Ornamental--Wisconsin. 3. Gardening--Minnesota. 4. Gardening--Wisconsin. I. Williamson, Don, 1962- II. Title.

SB453.2.M56E53 2006   635'.09776   C2005-906713-6

Scanning & Digital Film: Elite Lithographers Co.

Front cover photographs: Outside edge, clockwise from top right: Blanc Double de Coubert rose *(Tamara Eder);* iris *(Tamara Eder);* sweet pea *(Tim Matheson);* Morden Sunrise rose *(Tamara Eder);* lily *(Laura Peters);* dahlia *(Tim Matheson);* lily *(Erika Flatt).* Middle section, top to bottom: crabapple *(Tim Matheson);* lilac *(Tamara Eder);* fringe tree *(Tim Matheson).*

Photography: All photos by **Tamara Eder, Tim Matheson** and **Laura Peters** except:
AAFC 127b; **AgCanada** 124a&b; **Bailey Nurseries-Michelle Meyer** 121; **J.C. Bakker & Sons** 125a; **Sandra Bit** 146a; **David Cavagnaro** 20a, 31b; **Chicagoland Grows Inc.** 81a; **Janet Davis** 127a; **Joan de Grey** 47a; **Don Doucette** 110b; **Jen Fafard** 145a; **Derek Fell** 31a, 45b; **Erika Flatt** 9b, 38a, 93a, 111b, 141b, 165b; **Anne Gordon** 20b, 44b, 91a&b, 136b; **Horticolor** 131b; **Duncan Kelbaugh** 141a; **Dawn Loewen** 67a, 78a, 82a; **Debra Knapke** 44a; **Marilynn McAra** 145b; **Kim O'Leary** 25a&b, 140a, 143a, 152b; **Allison Penko** 49a, 54a, 58a, 68a, 73b, 80a, 92b, 94b, 102a&b, 105a&b, 109b, 130b, 140b, 144a, 158a, 161a&b, 163a, 164b; **Photos.com** 147a; **Robert Ritchie** 8b, 43b, 56a&b, 76c, 101a, 107b, 123a&b, 126a, 152a; **Leila Sidi** 147b; **Joy Spurr** 128a, 131a; **Peter Thompstone** 50a, 61a&b; **Mark Turner** 103a; **Don Williamson** 142a&b, 149a; **Tim Wood** 76a&b, 94a, 110a, 138a.

PC: P13

Table of Contents

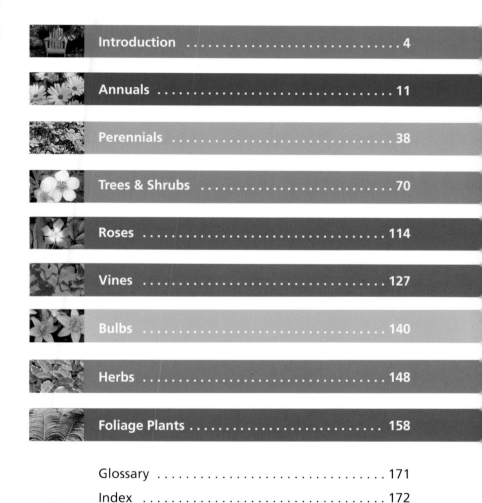

Introduction 4

Annuals 11

Perennials 38

Trees & Shrubs 70

Roses 114

Vines 127

Bulbs 140

Herbs 148

Foliage Plants 158

Glossary 171
Index 172
About the Authors & Acknowledgments 176

Introduction

Starting a garden can seem like a daunting task. Which plants should you choose? Where in the garden should you put them? This book is intended to give beginning gardeners the information they need to start planning and planting gardens of their own. It describes a wide variety of plants and provides basic planting information such as where and how to plant.

Minnesota and Wisconsin exhibit a wide diversity of ecological regions, and each presents its own unique challenges. One of the biggest challenges is selecting plants that can handle our climate, especially our cold winters. USDA hardiness zones are based on how cold it gets in the winter. Plants are rated based on the zones in which they grow successfully, but cold is not the only factor influencing winter survival. A winter temperature of -15° F is very different with snow cover than without; in soggy soil or in dry; following a hot summer or a long, cold, wet one. These factors will have more influence on the survival of plants than temperature will.

Spring and fall frost dates are often used when discussing climate and gardening. They give us a general idea of when the last chance of frost is in spring and the first chance of frost is in fall. The last-frost date in spring combined with the first-frost date in fall allows us to predict the length of the growing season. Your local garden center should be able to provide you with local hardiness zones and frost date information.

Getting Started

When planning your garden, start with a quick analysis of the garden as it is now. Plants have different requirements and it is easier to put the right plant in the right place rather than to change growing conditions in your yard to suit the plants you want.

Knowing which parts of your yard receive the most and least amounts of sunlight will help you to choose the proper plants and decide where to plant them. Light is classified into four basic groups: full sun (direct, unobstructed light all or most of the day); partial sun (direct sun for about half the day and shade for the rest); light shade (shade all or most of the day with some sun filtering through to ground level); and full shade (no direct sunlight). Most plants prefer a specific amount of light, but many can adapt to a range of light levels.

Plants use the soil to hold themselves upright, but also rely on the many resources it holds: air, water, nutrients, organic matter and a host of microbes. The particle size of the soil influences the amount of air, water and nutrients it can hold. Sand, with the largest particles, has a lot of air space and allows water and nutrients to drain quickly. Clay, with the smallest particles, is high in nutrients but has very little air space. Water is therefore slow to penetrate clay and slow to drain from it.

Soil acidity or alkalinity (measured on the pH scale) influences the nutrients available to plants. A pH of 7 is neutral; a lower pH is more acidic. Most plants prefer a soil with a pH of 5.5–7.5. Soil-testing kits are available at most garden centers, and soil samples can be sent to testing facilities for a more thorough analysis.

Compost is one of the best and most important amendments you can add to any type of soil. Compost improves soil by adding organic matter and nutrients, introducing soil microbes, increasing water retention and improving drainage. Compost can be purchased, or you can make it in your own backyard.

Microclimates are small areas that are generally warmer or colder than the

USDA Hardiness Zones Map

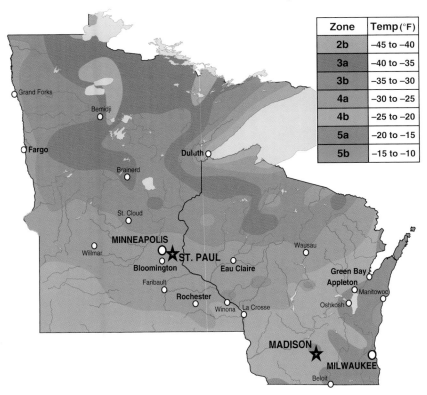

Zone	Temp (°F)
2b	−45 to −40
3a	−40 to −35
3b	−35 to −30
4a	−30 to −25
4b	−25 to −20
5a	−20 to −15
5b	−15 to −10

surrounding area. Buildings, fences, trees and other large structures can provide extra shelter in winter, but may trap heat in summer, thus creating a warmer micro-climate. The bottoms of hills are usually colder than the tops, but may not be as windy. Take advantage of these areas when you plan your garden and choose your plants; you may even grow out-of-zone plants successfully in a warm, sheltered location.

Selecting Plants

It's important to purchase healthy plants that are free of pests and diseases. Such plants will establish quickly in your garden and won't introduce problems that may spread to other plants. You should have a good idea of what the plant is supposed to look like—the color and shape of the leaves and the habit of the plant—and then inspect the plant for signs of disease or infestation.

The majority of plants are container-grown. This is an efficient way for nurseries and greenhouses to grow plants, but when plants grow in a restricted space for too long, they can become pot bound with their roots densely encircling the inside of the pot. Avoid purchasing plants in this condition; they are often stressed and can take longer to establish. In some cases they may not establish at all. It is often possible to remove pots temporarily to look at the condition of the roots. You can check for soil-borne insects and rotten roots at the same time.

Planting Basics

The following tips apply to all plants:

- Prepare the garden before planting. Dig over the soil, pull up any weeds and make any needed amendments before you begin planting, if possible. This may be more difficult in established beds to which you want to add a single plant. The prepared area should be at least twice the size of the plant you want to put in, and preferably the expected size of the mature plant.

- Settle the soil with water when planting. Good contact between the roots and the soil is important, but if you press the soil down too firmly, as often happens when you step on the soil, you can cause compaction, which reduces the movement of water through the soil and leaves very few air spaces. Instead, pour water in as you fill the hole with soil. The water will settle the soil evenly without allowing it to compact.

- Unwrap the roots. Remove any container before planting. In particular, you should remove fiber pots, wire cages and burlap before planting trees. Fiber pots decompose very slowly, if at all, and wick moisture away from the plant. Synthetic burlap won't decompose, and wire cages can strangle the roots as they mature. The only exceptions to this rule are true peat pots and pellets used to start annuals and vegetables; these decompose and can be planted with the young transplants.

Gently remove container.

Ensure proper planting depth.

Backfill with soil.

- Accommodate the rootball. If you prepared your planting area ahead of time, the hole will only need to be big enough to accommodate the rootball with the roots spread out slightly. We suggest preparing a large area for any tree or shrub planting by loosening the soil with a power tiller or garden fork, well out from the planting hole.
- Know the mature size. Place your plants based on how big the plants will grow rather than how big they are when you plant them. Large plants should have enough room to mature without interfering with walls, roof overhangs, power lines and walkways.
- Plant at the same depth in the soil. Plants generally like to grow at a specific level in relation to the soil and should be planted at the same level they were growing at before you transplanted them.
- Identify your plants. Keep track of what's what in your garden by putting a tag next to your plant when you plant it, or by making an overhead drawing with plant names and locations. It's very easy for beginning gardeners to forget exactly what they planted and where they planted it.
- Water deeply and infrequently. It's better to water deeply once every week or two rather than to water lightly more often. Deep watering forces roots to grow as they search for water and helps them survive dry spells when water bans may restrict your watering regimen. Always check the root zone before you water. New gardeners tend to overwater annuals and perennials and underwater trees and shrubs.

Annuals

Annuals are planted new each year and are only expected to last for a single growing season. Their flowers and decorative foliage provide bright splashes of color and can fill in spaces around immature trees, shrubs and perennials.

Annuals are easy to plant and are usually sold in small packs of four or six. The roots quickly fill the space in these small packs, so the small rootball should be broken up before planting. For most annuals, split the ball in two up the center, or run your thumb up each side to break up the roots.

Many annuals are grown from seed and can be started directly in the garden. Some plants dislike their roots being disturbed, and these plants are often grown directly from seed or grown in peat pots or pellets to minimize root disturbance. Consult an annual book such as Lone Pine's *Annuals for Minnesota and Wisconsin* for further information on the care and growing of annuals.

Perennials

Perennials grow for three or more years. Herbaceous perennials usually die back to the ground each fall and send up new shoots in spring, though some are ever-

Settle backfilled soil with water.

Water the plant well.

Add a layer of mulch.

green. They often have a shorter period of bloom than annuals, but require less care.

Many perennials benefit from being divided every few years. This keeps them growing and blooming vigorously, and in some cases controls their spread. Dividing involves digging up the plant, removing dead bits, breaking the plant into several pieces and replanting some or all of the pieces. Extra pieces can be given as gifts to family, friends and neighbors. Consult a perennial book such as Lone Pine's *Perennials for Minnesota and Wisconsin* for further information on the care of perennials.

Trees and Shrubs

Trees and shrubs provide the bones of the garden. They are often the slowest growing plants, but usually live the longest. Characterized by leaf type, they may be deciduous or evergreen, and needled or broad-leaved.

Trees should have as little disturbed soil as possible at the bottom of the planting hole. Loose dirt settles over time and sinking even an inch can kill some trees.

Staking, sometimes recommended for newly planted trees, is only necessary for trees over 5' tall.

Pruning is more often required for shrubs than trees. It helps them maintain

Roses are lovely on their own or in mixed borders.

an attractive shape and can improve blooming. It is a good idea to take a pruning course or to hire or consult with an ISA (International Society of Arboriculture) certified arborist if you have never pruned before. Consult Lone Pine's *Tree and Shrub Gardening for Minnesota and Wisconsin* for information about pruning trees and shrubs.

Roses

Roses are beautiful shrubs with lovely, often-fragrant, blooms. Traditionally, most roses only bloomed once in the growing season, but new varieties bloom all, or almost all, summer.

Generally, roses prefer a fertile, well-prepared planting area. A rule of thumb is to prepare an area 24" across, front to back and side to side, and 24" deep. Add plenty of compost or other fertile organic matter and keep roses well watered during the growing season. Many roses are quite durable and will adapt to poorer conditions. Roses, like all shrubs, have specific pruning requirements.

Vines

Vines or climbing plants are useful for screening and shade, especially in a location too small for a tree. They may be

Annuals are great for blasts of color in summer.

Virginia creeper provides beautiful red fall color.

woody or herbaceous, and annual or perennial.

Most vines need sturdy supports to grow up on. Trellises, arbors, porch railings, fences, walls, poles and trees are all possible supports. If a support is needed, ensure it's in place before you plant to avoid disturbing the roots later.

Basically, any plant that covers the ground can be used as a groundcover. Groundcovers are often spreading plants with dense growth that are used to control soil erosion, to keep weeds at bay, and to fill garden areas that are difficult to maintain. Groundcovers can be herbaceous or woody, and annual or perennial.

Vines and plants that are aggressive spreaders make excellent groundcovers, but any plant with dense growth, planted in multiple numbers, will serve the purpose. Space plants closer together when planting to ensure the ground is completely covered.

Bulbs
These plants have fleshy underground storage organs that allow them to survive extended periods of dormancy. They are often grown for the bright splashes of color their flowers provide. They may be spring, summer or fall flowering.

Hardy bulbs can be left in the ground and will flower every year, but many popular tender plants grow from bulbs, corms or tubers. These tender plants are generally lifted from the garden in fall as the foliage dies back, and are stored in a cool, frost-free location for winter, to be replanted in spring.

Herbs
Herbs may be medicinal or culinary and are often both. A few common culinary herbs are listed in this book. Even if you don't cook with herbs, the often-fragrant foliage adds its aroma to the garden and the plants have decorative forms, leaves and flowers.

Many herbs have pollen-producing flowers that attract butterflies, bees and hummingbirds. They also attract predatory insects. These useful insects help to manage your pest problems by feasting on problem insects such as aphids, mealy bugs and whiteflies.

Foliage Plants
Foliage is an important consideration when choosing plants for your garden.

Lilies have colorful summer blooms.

Herbs are attractive and useful garden plants.

Although many plants look spectacular in bloom, they can seem rather dull without flowers. Including a variety of plants with unique, interesting or striking foliage can provide all the color and texture you want without the need to rely on flowers.

Ornamental grasses are becoming very popular garden additions. Grasses offer a variety of textures and foliage colors, and at least three seasons of interest. There is an ornamental grass for every

Include plants with striking foliage in your garden.

garden situation and condition. Some grasses will thrive in any garden condition, including hot and dry to cool and wet, and in all types of soils.

Ornamental grasses have very few insect or disease problems. They require very little maintenance other than cutting the perennial grasses back in fall or spring. Ornamental grasses add winter interest and overwinter much better in our cold, northern climate if they are cut back in spring.

Ferns are ancient plants that have adapted to many different environments. The fern family is a very large group of plants with interesting foliage in a wide array of shapes and colors. Ferns do not produce flowers, but instead reproduce by spores borne in structures on the undersides and margins of the foliage. Ferns are generally planted in moist, shaded gardens, but some will thrive in dry shade under the deep shade of some trees, such as beech and magnolia.

We have included a variety of plants grown for their foliage throughout the book. Many annuals, perennials, trees, shrubs, vines and herbs have wonderful foliage, and will be an asset to your garden landscape.

Final Comments

We encourage you to visit the outstanding garden shows, county fairs, public gardens, arboretums and private gardens we have here in Wisconsin and Minnesota to see which plants grow best, and if any plants catch your interest. A walk through your neighborhood is also a grand way to see what plants might do well in your own garden. Don't be afraid to ask questions.

Also, don't be afraid to experiment. No matter how many books you read, trying things yourself is the best way to learn and to find out what will grow in your garden. Use the information provided as guidelines, then have fun!

Ageratum
Ageratum

With their soft, globular, fuzzy blooms and often diminutive size, ageratums are one of the most popular edging plants.

Growing

Ageratum prefers **full sun** but tolerates partial shade. The soil should be **fertile, moist** and **well drained**. A moisture-retaining mulch will prevent the soil from drying out excessively. Don't mulch too thickly or too close to the base of the plant, or it may develop crown rot or root rot. Adequate fertilization is required to keep ageratum blooming throughout summer. Deadhead to prolong blooming and to keep plants looking tidy.

Tips

The smaller varieties, which become almost completely covered with the fluffy flowerheads, make excellent edging plants for flowerbeds. They are also attractive grouped in masses or grown in planters. The taller varieties are useful in the center of a flowerbed and make interesting cut flowers.

Recommended

A. houstonianum forms a large, leggy mound that can grow up to 24" tall, though many cultivars have been developed that have a low, bushy habit and generally grow between 6–12" tall. **Artist Hybrids** are compact, mounding plants 8–12" tall, with plentiful flowers that continue blooming throughout summer. '**Blue Hawaii**' is a compact plant, 6–12" tall, with blue flowers.

Also called: floss flower **Features:** fuzzy, blue, purple, white, pink, burgundy flowers; mounded habit **Height:** 6–36" **Spread:** 10–14"

A. *houstonianum* 'Blue Hawaii' (above),
A. *houstonianum* (below)

The genus name, Ageratum, *is from the Greek, meaning 'without age,' and refers to the long-lasting flowers.*

Begonia

Begonia

B. Rex Cultorum Hybrid 'Escargot' (above), B. × tuberhybrida (below)

Begonia encompasses a large family of wonderful, versatile plants featuring lovely blooms and stellar foliage.

Growing

Begonias grow best in **light or partial shade** in **fertile, well-drained, neutral to acidic** soil **rich in organic matter.** Some wax begonias tolerate sun if the soil is kept moist. Allow the soil to dry out slightly between waterings, particularly for tuberous begonias. Don't plant begonias before the soil warms in spring; in cold soil they may fail to thrive. Plant tubers concave side up.

Tips

Begonias are useful for shaded garden beds and planters. Trailing tuberous varieties look great when their flowers are allowed to cascade down. Wax begonias are attractive as edging plants. Rex begonias, with their dramatic foliage, and DRAGON WING are useful as specimen plants.

Recommended

B. × *hybrida* DRAGON WING bears deep scarlet to deep pink flowers and angel-winged foliage. It is heat tolerant.

B. Rex Cultorum **Hybrids** (rex begonias) are grown for their dramatic, colorful foliage.

B. semperflorens (wax begonias) have pink, white, red or bicolored flowers and green, bronze, reddish or white-variegated foliage.

B. × *tuberhybrida* (tuberous begonias) are generally sold as tubers. The wonderful flowers come in many shades of red, pink, yellow, orange or white.

Features: pink, white, red, yellow, orange, bicolored, picotee flowers; decorative foliage; easy to grow; low maintenance **Height:** 6–24" **Spread:** 6–24"

Black-Eyed Susan
Rudbeckia

R. hirta 'Becky Mixed' (above), *R. hirta* (below)

*I*t's hard to name a better annual than *Rudbeckia* for providing dynamic color from mid-summer to frost.

Growing

Black-eyed Susan grows equally well in **full sun** or **partial shade**. The soil should be of **average fertility, humus rich, moist** and **well drained**. This plant tolerates heavy clay soil and hot weather. If it is growing in loose, moist soil, black-eyed Susan may reseed itself. Plants can be purchased and started from seed early indoors or directly sown in the garden around the last-frost date. Deadhead to prolong blooming.

Tips

Plant black-eyed Susan individually or in groups. Use it in beds and borders, large containers, meadow plantings and wildflower gardens. This plant will bloom well, even in the hottest part of the garden. Black-eyed Susan makes a long-lasting vase flower.

Recommended

R. hirta forms a bristly mound of foliage and bears bright yellow, daisy-like flowers with brown centers in summer and fall. A wide variety of cultivars are available, including dwarf plants and double-flowered plants.

This plant's tolerance for heavy soils makes it useful in new developments where the topsoil is often very thin.

Also called: coneflower, gloriosa daisy **Features:** yellow, orange, red, brown, sometimes bicolored, flowers with brown or green centers **Height:** 8–36" or more **Spread:** 12–20"

Browallia
Browallia

B. speciosa 'White Troll' (above), *B. speciosa* (below)

One might say that every plant listed in this book has pretty flowers; ugly flowers don't survive long in the nursery trade. Still, it's always amazing to find a magnificent beauty such as browallia flowering so freely in a yard with little sun.

Growing
Browallia tolerates any light conditions from full sun to full shade, but flower production and color are best in **partial shade**. The soil should be **fertile** and **well drained**. Do not cover the seeds when seeding because they need light to germinate. They do not like the cold, so wait several weeks after the last frost before setting out the plants. Pinch tips often to encourage new growth and more blooms.

Tips
Grow browallia in mixed borders, mixed containers or hanging baskets.

Recommended
B. speciosa forms a bushy mound of foliage and bears white, blue or purple flowers all summer. 'Garden Leader Blue' has deep blue flowers. **Jingle Bells Hybrids** include 'Blue Bells,' 'Jingle Bells Mix' and 'Silver Bells.' '**Starlight**' forms a compact mound bearing light blue, bright blue, purple or white flowers. The **Troll Series** plants are compact and bushy.

Browallia is generally problem free.

Features: abundant, purple, blue, white flowers; attractive foliage; easy to grow
Height: 6–18" **Spread:** 8–18"

Calendula
Calendula

C. officinalis 'Apricot Surprise' (above), *C. officinalis* (below)

If it's color you're after—color that can be seen a block away—you'll enjoy a long relationship with calendula.

Growing

Calendula does equally well in **full sun** or **partial shade** in **well-drained** soil of **average fertility**. It prefers cool weather and can withstand a light frost. Young plants are sometimes hard to find in nurseries. Calendula is easy to start from seed and that is how most gardeners grow it. A second sowing in mid-summer gives a good fall display. Deadhead to prolong blooming and to keep plants looking neat.

Tips

This informal plant looks attractive in annual and mixed borders and containers, and fits easily into the vegetable patch. It makes an excellent cut flower and works well in cottage gardens and large, informal beds. Calendula looks great planted in a swath of five or more.

Recommended

C. officinalis is a vigorous, tough, upright plant that bears daisy-like, single or double flowers in a wide range of yellow and orange shades. Several cultivars are available. It is a cold-hardy annual and often continues flowering until the ground freezes completely.

Calendula flowers are popular kitchen herbs that can be added to stews for color, or to salads for flavoring.

Also called: pot marigold, English marigold
Features: cream, yellow, gold, orange, apricot flowers; long blooming period; very easy to grow **Height:** 10–24" **Spread:** 8–20"

Celosia
Celosia

C. argentea Plumosa Group (above), C. argentea Cristata Group (below)

$\mathcal{T}$he fiery plumes of celosia are a favorite of many gardeners.

To dry celosia, pick the flowers when they are at their peak and hang them upside down in a cool, shaded place.

Growing
Celosia prefers a **sheltered** spot in **full sun**. The soil should be **fertile, moist** and **well drained**, with plenty of **organic matter** worked in.

Celosia grows best when directly sown in the garden. If starting indoors, seed in peat pots or pellets and plant them; if they are nursery-purchased plants, plant them before they begin to flower. Keep seeds moist while they are germinating and do not cover them.

Tips
Celosia works well in borders and beds as well as planters. The flowers make interesting additions to arrangements, either fresh or dried. The crested varieties work well as accents and as cut flowers.

Recommended
C. argentea is the species from which both the crested and plume-type cultivars have been developed. **Cristata Group** (crested celosia) has blooms that resemble brains or rooster combs. **Plumosa Group** (plume celosia) has feathery, plume-like blooms. Both groups have many varieties and cultivars.

C. spicata (*C. argentea* Spicata Group; wheat celosia) produces spike-like clusters of pink to rose flowers, often with a metallic sheen.

Also called: cockscomb, woolflower
Features: intensely colorful, interesting, red, orange, gold, yellow, pink or purple flowers **Height:** 6"–4' **Spread:** equal to or slightly less than height

Cleome
Cleome

*N*orthern gardeners caught on long ago to the special allure and charm of cleome, and it remains highly visible in gardens across Wisconsin and Minnesota.

Growing
Cleome prefers **full sun** but tolerates partial shade. It **adapts to most soils.** Mix in **organic matter** to help retain soil moisture. These plants are drought tolerant but perform best with regular watering. Pinch out the tip of the center stem on young plants to encourage branching and more blooms. Deadhead to prolong blooming and to reduce prolific self-seeding.

Tips
Cleome can be planted in groups at the back of a border or in the center of an island bed. It makes an attractive addition to a large, mixed container.

Recommended
C. hassleriana is a tall, upright plant with strong, supple, thorny stems. The foliage and flowers of this plant have a strong, but not unpleasant, scent. **'Helen Campbell'** has white flowers. **Royal Queen Series** has flowers in all colors. Plants in this series resist fading. **'Sparkler Blush'** is a dwarf cultivar that bears pink flowers that fade to white.

C. **'Linde Armstrong'** is a compact, thornless variety with rosy pink blooms. It is very heat tolerant and well suited to container growing.

Cleome provides hummingbirds with nectar well into fall.

C. hassleriana (above & below)

Also called: spider flower **Features:** attractive, scented foliage; purple, pink, white flowers; thorny stems **Height:** 10"–5' **Spread:** 18–36"

Coleus

Solenostemon (Coleus)

S. scutellarioides mixed cultivars (above & below)

Coleus is one of the most valuable annuals available for those less-than-sunny spots.

Try taking coleus cuttings from a mother plant and overwintering them inside. The cuttings root easily in a glass of water.

Growing

Coleus prefers **light shade** or **partial shade** but tolerates full shade if it isn't too dense, and full sun if the plants are watered regularly. The soil should be **average to fertile, humus rich, moist** and **well drained**.

Place the seeds in a refrigerator for one or two days before planting them on the soil surface; the cold temperatures help the seeds break dormancy. The seeds need light to germinate. The seedlings are green at first, but leaf variegation develops as the plants mature.

Tips

Coleus looks dramatic when grouped in beds, borders and mixed containers, or when planted as edging.

Pinch off flower buds once they have developed. Coleus flowers tend to stretch out and become less attractive after they bloom.

Recommended

S. scutellarioides (*Coleus blumei* var. *verschaffeltii*) forms a bushy mound of multi-colored, slightly toothed to very ruffled foliage. Dozens of cultivars are available, but many cannot be started from seed. New varieties that tolerate full sun and have larger, more colorful foliage are also available.

Features: brightly colored foliage **Height:** 6–36" or more **Spread:** usually equal to height

Cosmos

Cosmos

$\mathscr{F}$ew flowers, annual or perennial, throw such a riotous party
of color and form as cosmos.

Growing
Cosmos like **full sun** and **well-drained**
soil of **poor to average fertility**. Plant
out after the last frost. Overfertilizing
and overwatering can reduce the
number of flowers. Cut faded blooms
to encourage more buds. These plants
often self-seed.

Tips
Cosmos are attractive in cottage
gardens, at the backs of borders and
mass planted in informal beds and
borders.

To avoid staking, plant cosmos against
a fence or in a sheltered location, or
grow shorter varieties. Push twiggy
branches into the ground when the
plants are young and allow them to
grow up between the branches. The
mature plant will hide the branches.

C. bipinnatus (above), *C. bipinnatus* cultivar (below)

Recommended
C. atrosanguineus (chocolate cosmos) is an
upright plant with fragrant, dark maroon
flowers that some claim smell like chocolate.

C. bipinnatus (annual cosmos) is an erect
plant with fine, fern-like foliage. It, along
with its many cultivars, bears magenta, rose,
pink, white or bicolored flowers, usually
with yellow centers.

C. sulphureus (yellow cosmos) is a smaller,
denser plant than *C. bipinnatus* and has
gold, orange, scarlet or yellow flowers. Sow
directly in the garden. Many cultivars are
available.

Features: magenta, rose, pink, purple, white, yellow,
orange, scarlet flowers; fern-like foliage; easy to grow;
low maintenance **Height:** 1–7' **Spread:** 12–18"

Dahlberg Daisy
Thymophylla

T. tenuiloba (above & below)

Busy gardeners who like the look of the classic, yellow daisy but who would love to take the easy way out should grow Dahlberg daisies. They can handle poor soil and overall abuse, and sometimes that's a noble thing.

Growing
Dahlberg daisy prefers **full sun** in **well-drained** soil of **poor to average fertility**, but any well-drained soil is suitable. It prefers cool summers. In hot climates, it flowers in spring.

This cheerful annual rarely suffers from pest or disease problems.

Direct-sowed plants may not flower until quite late in summer. For earlier blooms, start the seeds indoors. Don't cover the seeds; they require light to germinate. Dahlberg daisy may self-sow and reappear each year.

Trim your plants back when flowering seems to be slowing to encourage new growth and more blooms, particularly when the weather cools.

Tips
Dahlberg daisy looks wonderful in any location where it can cascade over and trail down an edge. Use it along the edges of borders, along the tops of rock walls or in hanging baskets or mixed containers.

Recommended
T. tenuiloba (*Dyssodia tenuiloba*) forms a mound of ferny foliage. It produces many bright yellow, daisy-like flowers from spring until the summer heat causes them to fade.

Also called: golden fleece **Features:** bright yellow or, less commonly, orange flowers; fragrant foliage; easy to grow **Height:** 6–12" **Spread:** 12"

Dusty Miller
Senecio

S. cineraria 'Cirrus' (above), S. cineraria (below)

As one advances as a gardener, one learns that plant foliage is worth as much consideration as flower size, shape and color. Dusty miller is a classic case in point. Its magnificent silver-white foliage does a wonderful job of breaking up the overpowering green of most other plants.

Growing

Dusty miller prefers **full sun** but tolerates light shade. The soil should be of **average fertility** and **well drained**.

Tips

The soft, silvery, lacy leaves of dusty miller are its main feature, and it is used primarily as an edging plant. It is also used in beds, borders and containers. The silvery foliage makes a good backdrop to show off the brightly colored flowers of other plants.

Pinch off the flowers before they bloom. They aren't showy and they steal energy that would otherwise go to producing more foliage.

Recommended

S. cineraria forms a mound of fuzzy, silvery gray, lobed or finely divided foliage. Many cultivars have been developed with impressive foliage colors and shapes.

Mix dusty miller with geraniums, begonias or cockscombs to bring out the vibrant colors of those flowers.

Features: silvery foliage; neat habit; easy to grow **Height:** 12–24" **Spread:** equal to height or slightly narrower

Geranium

Pelargonium

P. peltatum cultivars (above & below)

The popularity of geraniums has prompted breeders to produce many new varieties that feature fabulous new colors, sizes, forms and fragrances. The Fireworks Series is a must-grow—it has brilliant flower colors *plus* outstanding foliage.

Growing

Geraniums prefer **full sun** but tolerate partial shade, though they may not bloom as profusely. The soil should be **fertile** and **well drained**.

Deadheading is essential to keep geraniums blooming and looking neat.

Tips

Geraniums are very popular for borders, beds, planters, hanging baskets and window boxes. Plant scented geraniums where they can be smelled as well as seen.

Recommended

P. × hortorum (zonal geranium) is a bushy plant with red, pink, purple, orange or white flowers and, frequently, banded or multi-colored foliage. Many cultivars are available.

P. peltatum (ivy-leaved geranium) has thick, waxy leaves and a trailing habit. Many cultivars are available.

P. **species** and **cultivars** (scented geraniums, scented pelargoniums) are a large group of geraniums that have scented leaves. The scents are grouped into the categories of rose, mint, citrus, fruit, spice and pungent.

Geraniums are perennials that are treated as annuals and can be kept indoors over winter in a bright room.

Features: red, pink, violet, orange, salmon, white, purple flowers; decorative or scented foliage; variable habits **Height:** 8–36" **Spread:** 6"–4'

Heliotrope
Heliotropium

H. arborescens (above & below)

Heliotrope was a favorite of well-heeled English gardeners who were busy creating the great formal gardens of the Victorian era. A single plant in a properly sized pot allows the timeless beauty of heliotrope to adorn any sunny spot on your property.

Growing

Heliotrope grows best in **full sun** in **fertile, moist, well-drained** soil rich in **organic matter**. Overwatering will kill it. Heliotrope will also be slow to recover if left to dry to the point of wilting. Plants that are a little underwatered tend to have a stronger scent.

Plant heliotrope out after all danger of frost has passed. Protect plants if an unexpected late frost or cold snap should arrive.

Tips

Use heliotrope in containers or beds near windows and patios where the wonderful scent of the flowers can be enjoyed.

Recommended

H. arborescens is an upright, shrub-like plant featuring attractively veined foliage. Tiny bundles of soft violet, purple, blue or white flowers are produced all summer. Some new cultivars are not as strongly scented as the species. '**Atlantis**' and '**Nagano**' are very heat-tolerant selections that do well in containers and hanging baskets. '**Marine**' has violet-blue flowers.

Heliotrope requires little maintenance and its lovely scented blooms attract butterflies.

Also called: cherry pie plant **Features:** attractive foliage; abundant, purple, blue, white flowers; fragrance **Height:** 8"–4' **Spread:** 12–24"

Impatiens
Impatiens

I. walleriana (above), *I. hawkeri* (below)

*A*t the top of the list of shade-loving annuals we are all lucky to find impatiens. What other plant brings spirited, season-long color to the dark corners of our yards and gardens?

Growing

Impatiens does best in **partial shade** or **light shade** but tolerates full shade. Some tolerate full sun if kept moist. The soil should be **fertile, humus rich, moist** and **well drained**.

Tips

Impatiens grows and flowers profusely even in shade. Mass plant it in beds under trees, in porch planters or along shady fences or walls. It also looks lovely in hanging baskets.

Recommended

I. balsamina (balsam impatiens) blooms in shades of purple, red, pink or white. There are several double-flowered cultivars. This is the best impatiens for sun.

I. hawkeri (New Guinea Hybrids, New Guinea impatiens) flowers in shades of red, orange, pink, purple or white. The foliage is often variegated with a yellow stripe down the center of each leaf.

I. Seashell Series are compact plants with flowers in shades of yellow, orange, apricot or pink.

I. walleriana (impatiens, busy Lizzie) flowers in shades of purple, red, burgundy, pink, yellow, salmon, orange, apricot or white or can be bicolored. Dozens of cultivars are available.

Features: purple, red, burgundy, pink, yellow, salmon, orange, apricot, white, bicolored flowers; grows well in shade **Height:** 6–36" **Spread:** 8–24"

Lantana
Lantana

antanas that feature clusters of tiny orange and red flowers combine magically in pots with blue varieties of salvia, ageratum, browallia and lobelia.

Growing

Lantana grows best in **full sun** but tolerates partial shade. The soil should be **fertile, moist** and **well drained**. Plants are heat and drought tolerant. Cuttings can be taken in late summer and grown indoors for the winter so you will have plants the following summer.

Tips

Lantanas are tender shrubs that are grown as annuals. They make an attractive addition to beds and borders as well as mixed containers and hanging baskets.

L. camara 'Spreading Sunset' (above & below)

Recommended

L. camara is a bushy plant that bears round clusters of flowers in a variety of colors. The flowers often change color as they mature, giving flower clusters a striking, multi-colored appearance. **'Spreading Sunset'** bears brightly colored orange to red flowers.

L. **Patriot Series** has plants that flower in a wide range of colors and have minty, dark to mid-green foliage.

Lantanas are not intimidated by hot, dry weather, and a 3" bedding plant can reach the size of a small shrub in a single season.

Also called: shrub verbena **Features:** stunning yellow, orange, pink, purple, red, white flowers, often in combination; easy to grow; low maintenance **Height:** 2–42" **Spread:** 12–42"

Lavatera
Lavatera

L. trimestris 'Silver Cup' (above), L. cachemiriana (below)

Although only 25 species of Lavatera *exist, it is a diverse group of annuals, biennials, perennials and shrubs.*

Lavatera is a large, bushy annual with lovely, often richly veined, open flowers and attractive, maple-leaf-shaped foliage. *L. trimestris* is superb in the middle or to the rear of the garden bed.

Growing
Lavatera prefers **full sun** and **light, well-drained** soil of **average fertility**. It likes cool, moist weather, and appreciates some shade from the hot afternoon sun. Use peat pots when starting seeds indoors. Lavatera resents having its roots disturbed. Direct seeding is best. Plant out seedlings after last frost.

Stake tall varieties to keep them from falling over in summer rain.

Tips
This large, shrubby plant works well in beds and borders or behind smaller plants for a colorful backdrop. It also works well as a temporary hedge. The flowers can be used for cuttings and are edible.

Recommended
L. arborea (tree mallow) is a large plant with funnel-shaped, pinkish purple flowers.

L. cachemiriana is another large plant that bears light pink flowers.

L. trimestris is a bushy plant that bears red, pink, rose pink, salmon pink or white, funnel-shaped flowers. Cultivars are available.

Features: delicate, rose, pink, salmon, purple, white flowers; easy care; tough plant
Height: 18"–10' **Spread:** 18"–5'

Marigold
Tagetes

T. patula cultivars (above & below)

There are a huge number of marigolds to choose from, many offering far different flower styles from the stuffy, cushion-form that grandma grew. Some things have remained constant: marigolds are easy to grow, withstand heat and tolerate dry conditions.

Growing
Marigolds grow best in **full sun**. The soil should be of **average fertility** and **well drained**. These plants are drought tolerant and hold up well in windy, rainy weather. Deadhead to prolong blooming and to keep the plants tidy.

Tips
Mass planted or mixed with other plants, marigolds make a vibrant addition to beds, borders and container gardens. These plants will thrive in the hottest, driest parts of your garden.

Recommended
Many cultivars are available for all the species. *T. erecta* (African marigold, American marigold, Aztec marigold) is the largest plant with the biggest flowers; *T. patula* (French marigold) is low growing and has a wide range of flower colors; *T. tenuifolia* (signet marigold) has recently become more popular because of its feathery foliage and small, dainty flowers; *T.* **Triploid Hybrids** (triploid marigold) were developed by crossing French and African marigolds, which has resulted in plants with huge flowers and compact growth.

Features: bright yellow, red, orange, brown, gold, cream, bicolored flowers; fragrant foliage; easy to grow **Height:** 7–36" **Spread:** 12–24"

Osteospermum
Osteospermum

O. 'Lavender Mist' (above), *O. ecklonis* (below)

Osteospermums are outstanding when massed in the garden bed but possess an assured and stately nature that allows plants that are placed singly to hold their own. Their muted shades of color give the plants a subtle elegance.

You may find these plants listed as both Osteospermum *and* Dimorphotheca. *The latter is a closely related genus that used to include the species now listed as* Osteospermum.

Growing
Plant in **full sun** in **light, evenly moist, moderately fertile, well-drained** soil. Do not overwater or let the plants wilt. Feed osteospermums regularly to keep them flowering all summer long. Use an organic mulch to cut down on the plants' water needs. Deadhead to prolong flowering and to keep plants looking neat. Pinch young plants to encourage bushy growth.

Tips
Osteospermums are best used in containers or beds, and their daisy flowers look great mixed with other plants such as petunia or verbena.

Recommended
O. ecklonis is a subshrub with a variable habit, ranging from quite upright in form to a more prostrate habit. **Passion Mix** are free-flowering, heat-tolerant plants. **Starwhirls Series** have unique spoon-shaped petals.

O. **Symphony Series** are very heat tolerant, mounding plants.

Also called: African daisy, Cape daisy **Features:** attractive, orange, peach, yellow, pink, purple, lavender, white flowers, often with contrasting dark blue or purple centers **Height:** 10–20" **Spread:** 10–20"

Painted-Tongue
Salpiglossis

Painted-tongue is an up-and-coming firecracker of a flower that is being found at more and more nurseries across our two states. Its veined blooms are sure to attract attention.

Growing
Painted-tongue prefers **full sun** in **fertile, well-drained** soil **rich in organic matter**. A location **sheltered** from heavy rain and wind will keep them looking their best. These plants may fail in mid-summer heat, so grow them where they get a break from the intense, midday sun.

The seeds are very tiny and shouldn't be covered with soil. Keep them in a dark place until they sprout, then move the plants to a well-lit location.

Tips
Painted-tongue is useful in the middle or back of beds and borders. It can also be added to large, mixed containers.

Recommended
S. sinuata is an upright plant. **'Blue Peacock'** has blue flowers with yellow throats and dark veins. **Casino Series** comes in a wide range of colors, blooms early and tolerates rain and wind. The **Royale Series** has flowers with more pronounced veining in the throat.

Also called: velvet flower **Features:** red, blue, yellow, orange, purple, brown, often patterned, bicolored flowers **Height:** up to 24" **Spread:** 12"

S. sinuata cultivars (above & below)

The iridescent quality of these flowers causes their color to change as they move in a breeze.

Petunia
Petunia

P. milliflora type 'Fantasy' (above), P. multiflora type (below)

Long an old-fashioned mainstay of the American flower garden, grandma's dear petunias have received a real shot of adrenaline with the recent introduction of the Waves, Supertunias and Surfinias.

Growing
Petunias prefer **full sun**. The soil should be of **average to rich fertility, light, sandy** and **well drained**. Pinch halfway back in mid-summer to keep plants bushy and to encourage new growth and flowers.

For speedy growth, prolific blooming and ease of care, petunias are hard to beat.

Most of the newer varieties do not require the excessive deadheading that made the maintenance of petunias a chore, but thorough deadheading at least once a week is still a good idea.

Tips
Use petunias in beds, borders, containers and hanging baskets.

Recommended
P. × hybrida is a large group of popular, sun-loving annuals that fall into three categories: **grandifloras** have the largest flowers in the widest range of colors, but they can be damaged by rain; **multifloras** have smaller but more flowers than the grandifloras and can tolerate adverse weather conditions better; and **millifloras** have the smallest flowers in the narrowest range of colors, but this type is the most prolific and least likely to be damaged by heavy rain.

Features: pink, purple, red, white, yellow, coral, blue, bicolored flowers; versatile plants
Height: 6–18" **Spread:** 12–24" or wider

Polka Dot Plant
Hypoestes

Polka dot plant is enjoying a surge of popularity as a foliage plant as gardeners become increasingly aware that varied, attractive leaves are a key component of good garden design.

Growing
Polka dot plant prefers **full sun** but tolerates light shade. Too much shade will reduce leaf coloration and can encourage floppy growth. The soil should be of **average fertility, humus rich, moist** and **well drained**.

Seed indoors in early spring. Pinch the growing tips frequently to encourage bushy growth. Pinch off the inconspicuous flowers, or the plants may decline.

Tips
Polka dot plant can be used in small groups as an accent plant, in mass plantings and in mixed containers. In general, because this plant is small, it looks best when planted in clusters rather than singly.

Recommended
H. phyllostachya (*H. sanguinolenta*) is a bushy plant grown for its attractive foliage. This species has mostly green leaves that are lightly dusted with pink spots. Several cultivars have more dramatic foliage. **Confetti Series** foliage is heavily spotted with light or dark pink or white. **Splash Series** plants have foliage that is brightly streaked and spotted with pink, white or red.

Features: colorful, pink-, red- or white-spotted foliage **Height:** 12–24" **Spread:** 8–12"

H. phyllostachya 'Confetti' (above), *H. phyllostachya* 'Pink Splash' (below)

Polka dot plant is often grown as a houseplant and does best near a sunny window.

Salvia
Salvia

S. *splendens* (red) and S. *farinacea* (purple) with purple lobelia (all above), S. *viridis* (below)

isconsin and Minnesota gardeners know a good annual when they see it. Salvia has become a popular mainstay of beds, borders and containers across the two great states.

Growing

All salvia plants prefer **full sun** but tolerate light shade. The soil should be **moist** and **well drained** and of **average to rich fertility**, with a lot of **organic matter**.

The long-lasting flowers of salvias hold up well in adverse weather.

Tips

Salvias look good grouped in beds, borders and containers. The flowers are long lasting and make good cut flowers for arrangements.

To keep the plants producing flowers, water them often and fertilize monthly. Remove spent flowers before they begin to turn brown.

Recommended

The attractive and varied forms of salvia have something to offer every style of garden. There are a number of wonderful salvia species and cultivars. Two of the most popular are S. *farinacea* (mealy cup sage, blue sage), which has bright blue flowers clustered along stems powdered with silver, and S. *splendens* (salvia, scarlet sage), which is grown for its spikes of bright red, tubular flowers. Cultivars are available in white, pink, purple and orange.

Also called: sage **Features:** colorful, red, blue, purple, burgundy, pink, orange, salmon, yellow, cream, white, bicolored summer flowers; attractive foliage **Height:** 1–4' **Spread:** 8"–4'

Snapdragon
Antirrhinum

A. *majus* mixed cultivars (above), A. *majus* cultivar (below)

The rounded, playful spires of pastel flowers that define snapdragons have been popular in the northern U.S. almost since the land was settled.

Growing

Snapdragons prefer **full sun** but tolerate light or partial shade. The soil should be **fertile, rich in organic matter** and **well drained**. These plants prefer a **neutral or alkaline** soil and will not perform as well in acidic soil. Do not cover seeds when sowing because they require light for germination.

To encourage bushy growth, pinch the tips of the young plants. Cut off the flower spikes as they fade to promote further blooming and to prevent the plants from dying back before the end of the season.

Tips

The height of the variety dictates its place in the border—the shortest varieties work well near the front, and the tallest look good in the center or back. The dwarf and medium-height varieties can be used in planters. The trailing varieties do well in hanging baskets.

Recommended

There are many cultivars of *A. majus* available, generally grouped into four classes: dwarf, medium, giant and trailing.

Snapdragons can handle cold weather. They are a good choice for gardeners who can't wait for the last-frost date to plant their gardens.

Features: entertaining, white, cream, yellow, orange, red, maroon, pink, purple, bicolored summer flowers **Height:** 6"–4' **Spread:** 6–20"

Sweet Alyssum
Lobularia

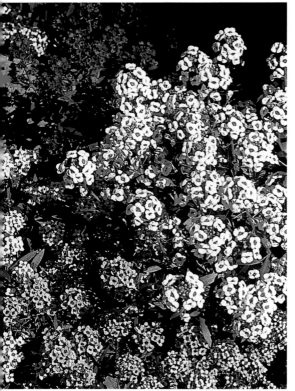

L. maritima cultivars (above & below)

Leave alyssum plants out all winter. In spring, remove the previous year's growth to expose self-sown seedlings below.

Sweet alyssum is one of the most popular and useful edging plants available to northern gardeners, and for many years has been a mainstay of the front of the garden bed.

Growing
Sweet alyssum prefers **full sun** but tolerates light shade. **Well-drained** soil of **average fertility** is preferred, but poor soil is tolerated. This plant dislikes having its roots disturbed, so if starting it indoors, use peat pots or pellets. Trim sweet alyssum back occasionally over the summer to keep it flowering and looking good.

Tips
Sweet alyssum creeps around rock gardens, over rock walls and along the edges of beds. It is an excellent choice for seeding into cracks and crevices of walkways and between patio stones, and once established it readily reseeds. Sweet alyssum is also good for filling in spaces between taller plants in borders and mixed containers.

Recommended
L. maritima forms a low, spreading mound of foliage. The entire plant appears to be covered in tiny blossoms when in full flower. Cultivars with flowers in a wide range of colors are available.

Features: fragrant, pink, purple, yellow, salmon, white flowers **Height:** 3–12" **Spread:** 6–24"

Verbena
Verbena

V. bonariensis (above), *V. × hybrida* (below)

Verbenas are exceptional plants in the north. Their colorful, mounding clusters of small flowers are the perfect foil for more erect, larger-flowered annuals.

Growing

Verbenas grow best in **full sun**. The soil should be **fertile** and very **well drained**. Pinch back young plants for bushy growth.

Tips

Use verbenas on rock walls and in beds, borders, rock gardens, containers, hanging baskets and window boxes. They make good substitutes for ivy-leaved geranium where the sun is hot and where a roof overhang keeps the mildew-prone verbenas dry.

Recommended

V. bonariensis forms a low clump of foliage from which tall, stiff stems emerge, bearing clusters of small, purple flowers. Butterflies love this plant.

V. canadensis is a low-growing, spreading plant that bears clusters of pink flowers from mid-summer to fall. **'Homestead Purple'** bears dark purple flowers and is mildew resistant.

V. × hybrida is a bushy plant that may be upright or spreading. It bears clusters of small flowers in a wide range of colors. Cultivars are available.

V. pedula **Superbena Series** are vigorous, upright to trailing plants with excellent mildew resistance. The large flowers bloom in intense shades of red, pink or purple.

Also called: garden verbena **Features:** red, pink, purple, blue, yellow, scarlet, silver, peach, white summer flowers, some with white centers **Height:** 4"–5' **Spread:** 10–36"

Violet
Viola

V. × *wittrockiana* cultivar (above), *V. tricolor* (below)

Undertake a regimen of regular deadheading and few plants will bloom for as long a period in northern gardens as violets.

Growing

Violets prefer **full sun** but tolerate partial shade. The soil should be **fertile, moist** and **well drained**. Violets do best in cool weather, and may die back completely in the summer heat.

The more flowers you pick, the more profusely the plants will bloom.

Tips

Violets can be used in beds, borders or containers, or can be mixed with spring-flowering bulbs. The varied color combinations of violets complement almost every other type of bedding plant.

Plant more violets in late summer and early fall to refresh tired and faded flowerbeds. Violets will often re-awaken in spring if left to go dormant in fall, allowing for early-spring flowers.

Recommended

V. cornuta (horned violet, viola) is a low-growing plant. It flowers in shades of blue, purple or white with the distinctive and charming 'face' pattern violets are known for.

V. tricolor (Johnny-jump-up) has purple, white or yellow flowers, usually in combination. Several varieties have flowers in a single color, often purple.

V. × *wittrockiana* (pansy) is available in a wide variety of solid, patterned, bicolored or multi-colored flowers with face-like markings in every size imaginable.

Features: blue, purple, red, orange, yellow, pink, white, multi-colored flowers; easy to grow; low maintenance
Height: 3–10" **Spread:** 4–16"

Zinnia

Zinnia

*Z*innias have a wide range of uses in both formal and informal gardens, in containers and as cut flowers.

Growing

Zinnias grow best in **full sun.** The soil should be **fertile, rich in organic matter, moist** and **well drained.** To avoid disturbing the roots when transplanting seedlings, start seeds in individual peat pots. Deadhead to prolong blooming and to keep plants looking neat.

Tips

Zinnias are useful in beds, borders, containers and cutting gardens. The dwarf selections can be used as edging plants. These plants provide wonderful fall color.

Recommended

Z. elegans is a bushy, upright plant with daisy-like flowers in a variety of forms. Heights vary from 6–36". Many cultivars are available.

Z. haageana 'Orange Star' (above), Z. elegans cultivars (below)

Z. haageana (Mexican zinnia) is a bushy plant with narrow leaves that bears bright, bicolored or tricolored, daisy-like flowers in shades of orange, red, yellow, maroon, brown or gold. It grows 12–24" tall. Cultivars are available.

Z. **Profusion Series** are fast-growing, mildew-resistant, compact hybrids. These All-America Selections winners bear bright, cherry red, orange or white flowers.

Mildew can be a problem for zinnias, so choose mildew-resistant cultivars, grow them in locations with good air circulation and avoid wetting the foliage.

Features: bushy plants; colorful flowers in shades of red, yellow, green, purple, orange, pink, white, maroon, brown, gold, some are bicolored or tricolored
Height: 6–36" **Spread:** 12"

Ajuga

Ajuga

A. reptans 'Pat's Selection' (above), A. reptans 'Caitlin's Giant' (below)

Growing

Ajugas develop the best leaf color in **partial or light shade** but tolerate full sun and full shade. The leaves may become scorched in direct sun. Any **well-drained** soil is suitable. Winter protection, such as mulch, is recommended if snow cover isn't dependable in your garden.

Divide these vigorous plants any time during the growing season. Remove any new growth or seedlings that don't show the hybrid leaf coloring.

Tips

Ajugas make excellent ground-covers for difficult sites, such as exposed slopes and dense shade. They are also attractive in shrub borders, where their dense growth will prevent the spread of all but the most tenacious weeds.

Whether scattered here and there alongside a shady stone path, or massed to create a billowy blanket in partial sun, ajuga will quickly become one of your favorite groundcovers.

Recommended

A. pyramidalis is a mound-forming perennial with deep to pale blue flowers borne in small pyramidal whorls along the top of the flowering stems. **'Metallica Crispa'** is a very slow-grow-ing plant with dense, crinkled, irides-cent foliage.

A. reptans is a low, quick-spreading groundcover. The many cultivars are grown for their colorful, often-variegated foliage.

Also called: bugleweed **Features:** colorful foliage; late-spring to early-summer blue flowers **Height:** 6–10" **Spread:** 12–24" **Hardiness:** zones 3–8

Artemisia
Artemisia

The silvery foliage of artemisias provides wonderful contrast and texture to the perennial border.

Growing
Artemisias grow best in **full sun**. The soil should be of **average to high fertility** and **well drained**. They dislike **wet, humid** conditions.

Artemisias respond well to pruning in late spring. If you prune before May, frost may kill any new growth. When plants look straggly, cut them back hard to encourage new growth and to maintain a neater form. Divide them every year or two when the plants thin out in their centers.

Tips
Use artemisias in rock gardens and borders. Their silvery gray foliage makes them good backdrop plants to use behind brightly colored flowers, or to fill in spaces between other plants. Smaller forms may be used to create knot gardens.

Recommended
A. absinthium (wormwood) is clump-forming and woody-based, and has aromatic, hairy, silvery gray foliage. (Zones 4–8)

A. ludoviciana (white sage, silver sage) cultivars are upright, clump-forming plants with silvery white foliage. (Zones 4–8)

A. stelleriana 'Silver Brocade' (above),
A. ludoviciana 'Valerie Finnis' (below)

A. schmidtiana (silvermound artemisia) is a low, dense, mound-forming perennial with feathery, hairy, silvery gray foliage. **'Nana'** grows only half the size of the species.

A. stelleriana **'Silver Brocade'** is a low, somewhat spreading cultivar with soft, pale gray leaves.

Also called: wormwood, sage
Features: silvery gray, feathery or deeply lobed foliage **Height:** 6"–6'
Spread: 6–36" **Hardiness:** zones 3–8

Aster

Aster

A. novi-belgii cultivar (above), A. novi-belgii (below)

Growing

Asters prefer **full sun** in **fertile, moist, well-drained** soil. They tolerate partial shade. Pinch or shear plants back in early summer to promote dense growth and to reduce disease problems. Use mulch in winter to protect plants from temperature fluctuations. Divide every two or three years to maintain vigor and to control spread.

Tips

Use asters in borders and cottage gardens, or naturalize them in wild gardens. The shorter asters serve well as single plantings. The very tall varieties look great in broad swaths at the rear of the bed.

Show us a garden that lacks vibrant, fresh blooms in late summer, and we'll show you a gardener who has not yet discovered the wonder of asters.

Recommended

Some *Aster* species have recently been reclassified under the genus *Symphyotrichum*. You may see both names at garden centers.

Asters are bushy, mound-forming plants. Smaller asters that grow up to 36" tall include *A. alpinus* (alpine aster), *A.* × *frikartii* (zones 4–9), *Symphyotrichum dumosum* (*Aster dumosus*; bushy aster; zones 4–9), *S. ericoides* (*A. ericoides*; heath aster) and *S. oolentangiensis* (*A. azureus*; *A. oolentangiensis*; sky blue aster). *S. oolentangiensis* can reach 5' in fertile soils. Taller asters (over 36") include *S. laeve* (*A. laevis*; smooth aster), *S. lateriflorum* (*A. lateriflorus*; calico aster) and *S. novae-angliae* (*A. novae-angliae*; New England aster).

Features: red, white, blue, purple, pink late-summer to mid-fall flowers, often with yellow centers
Height: 10"–5' **Spread:** 12–36" **Hardiness:** zones 3–9

Astilbe
Astilbe

Give astilbe what it needs then stand back and marvel at a perennial that has it all—refined, softly serrated foliage and graceful, bedazzling blooms.

Growing

Astilbes grow best in **light or partial shade** in **fertile, humus-rich, acidic, moist, well-drained** soil. They tolerate full shade, but with reduced flowering. Although they appreciate moist soil, astilbes don't like standing water. Use mulch in summer to keep the roots cool and moist. Divide every three years to maintain plant vigor.

Root masses may lift out of the soil as they mature. Add a layer of topsoil and mulch, or replant deeper if this occurs.

Tips

Astilbes can be grown near the edges of bog gardens and ponds, and in woodland gardens and shaded borders.

A. × arendsii cultivar (above), A. × arendsii 'Bressingham Beauty' (below)

Recommended

Many cultivars of all the following species are available.

A. × arendsii (astilbe, false spirea, Arend's astilbe) is a group of hybrids with wonderful flowers, and some have bronze foliage.

A. chinensis (Chinese astilbe) is a dense, vigorous perennial that tolerates dry soil better than other astilbe species.

A. japonica (Japanese astilbe) is a compact, clump-forming perennial that is rarely grown in favor of its cultivars.

A. simplicifolia bears glossy, deeply cut or lobed foliage and narrow clusters of star-shaped, white flowers.

Features: attractive foliage; white, pink, purple, peach, red summer flowers
Height: 10"–4' **Spread:** 8–36"
Hardiness: zones 3–9

Balloon Flower
Platycodon

P. grandiflorus (above & below)

When using these lovely flowers in arrangements, singe the cut ends with a lit match to prevent the milky white sap from running.

There are only a handful of perennials that are as elegant as *Platycodon*.

Growing
Balloon flower grows well in **full sun** or **partial shade**. The soil should be **average to fertile, light, moist** and **well drained**. This plant dislikes too wet a soil. The roots resent being disturbed so this plant should not need dividing. Shoots that sprout up around the plant can be gently removed and planted to propagate. Dead-head to prolong blooming and to keep plants looking neat.

Tips
Use balloon flower in borders, rock gardens and cottage gardens. It does not like being crowded by other plants, so give it plenty of room to spread.

Balloon flower sprouts late in the season. Mark its location to avoid accidentally damaging it before it sprouts the following spring.

Recommended
P. grandiflorus is an upright, clump-forming perennial. It bears blue or purple flowers in summer. Its cultivars tend to be lower growing and more rounded in habit, and may have white, pink, blue, purple or double flowers.

Features: blue, purple, pink, white summer flowers; attractive flower buds; habit
Height: 24–36" **Spread:** 12–18"
Hardiness: zones 3–8

Black-Eyed Susan
Rudbeckia

R. fulgida with *Echinacea* (above), *R. nitida* 'Herbstsonne' (below)

One of the most popular perennials across the upper Midwest, *Rudbeckia* is long-lived and easy to grow.

Growing
Black-eyed Susans grow well in **full sun** or **partial shade**. The soil should be of **average fertility** and **well drained**. Fairly heavy clay soils are tolerated. Regular watering is best, but established plants are drought tolerant. Divide in spring or fall every three to five years.

Tips
Use black-eyed Susans in wildflower and natural gardens, beds and borders. This prairie native looks best when massed across a large area, and it combines wonderfully with tall grasses and other sun-loving plants such as *Liatris* and *Echinacea*. Pinch the plants in June to make shorter, bushier stands.

Recommended
R. fulgida is an upright, spreading plant bearing orange-yellow flowers with brown centers. **Var. *sullivantii* 'Goldsturm'** bears large, bright, golden yellow flowers.

R. laciniata (cutleaf cone-flower) forms a large, open clump. The yellow flowers have green centers. **'Goldquelle'** has bright yellow, double flowers.

R. nitida (shining coneflower) **'Herbstsonne'** grows to 7' and has bright, golden yellow ray flowers with a green center.

Features: bright yellow, orange, red mid-summer to fall flowers with centers typically brown or green; attractive foliage; easy to grow **Height:** 18"–7' **Spread:** 12–36" **Hardiness:** zones 3–9

Boltonia
Boltonia

B. asteroides (above & below)

Boltonia is a tall, easy-to-grow, pest- and disease-free plant that blooms profusely for four weeks or more, and brightens the garden with fresh color late in the season.

Growing

Boltonia prefers **full sun** and **fertile, humus-rich, moist, well-drained** soil. It tolerates partial shade, adapts to less fertile soils and even tolerates some drought. Divide in fall or early spring when the clump is overgrown or dying out in the middle.

The stout stems rarely require staking. If plants grow too tall for your liking, cut stems back by one-third in June.

Tips

This large plant can be used in the middle or at the back of a mixed border, in a naturalized or cottage-style garden or near a pond or other water feature.

Recommended

B. asteroides is a large, upright perennial with narrow, grayish green leaves. It bears lots of white or slightly purple daisy-like flowers with yellow centers. 'Pink Beauty' has a looser habit and bears pale pink flowers. 'Snowbank' has a denser, more compact habit and bears more white flowers than the species.

Features: white, mauve, pink late-summer and fall flowers with yellow centers; easy to grow
Height: 3–6' Spread: up to 4'
Hardiness: zones 4–9

Bugbane
Cimicifuga

*M*any gardeners think that without full sun, growing tall, commanding perennials is not possible. Repeat after me: *sim-ih-siff-YOU-guh!* This is a true shade perennial that gives you vertical to the point of vertigo.

Growing

Bugbanes grow best in **partial or light shade** in **fertile, humus-rich, moist** soil. They may require support from a peony hoop. The roots resent being disturbed, so the plants should not be divided. Plants spread by rhizomes; small pieces of root can be carefully unearthed and replanted in spring if more plants are desired.

Tips

Bugbanes make attractive additions to an open woodland garden, shaded border or pondside planting. They don't compete well with tree roots or other vigorous-rooted plants. They are worth growing close to the house because the late-season flowers are wonderfully fragrant.

Recommended

C. racemosa (black snakeroot) is a clump-forming perennial with long-stemmed spikes of fragrant, creamy white flowers. *C. simplex* (Kamchatka bugbane) is a clump-forming perennial with fragrant bottlebrush-like spikes of flowers. Cultivars of both species are available, including those with bronze or purple foliage.

C. simplex 'Brunette' (above), *C. racemosa* (below)

The botanists are at it again! Plants in the genus Cimicifuga *have been recently reclassified, and may now be found as belonging to the genus* Actaea.

Also called: snakeroot **Features:** fragrant, white, cream, pink late-summer and fall flowers; some plants have bronze or purple foliage **Height:** 2–7' **Spread:** 24" **Hardiness:** zones 3–8

Campanula
Campanula

C. persicifolia (above), C. carpatica 'White Clips' (below)

Growing

Campanulas grow well in **full sun, partial shade** or **light shade**. The soil should be of **average fertility** and **well drained**. They appreciate mulch to keep their roots cool and moist in summer and protected in winter, particularly if snow cover is inconsistent. Deadhead to prolong blooming.

Tips

Plant upright and mounding campanulas in borders and cottage gardens. Use low, spreading and trailing campanulas in rock gardens and on rock walls. You can also edge beds with the low-growing varieties.

Divide campanulas every few years, in early spring or late summer, to keep the plants vigorous and to prevent them from becoming invasive.

Few perennials offer the wide range of color, bloom types, heights and forms as do the campanulas. *C. glomerata* 'Superba,' is one of the most bedazzling perennials available to northern gardeners.

Recommended

Many species, cultivars and hybrids of campanula are available, with growth habits ranging from low and spreading to upright and trailing. The most common campanula is *C. carpatica* (Carpathian bellflower), a spreading, mounding perennial bearing blue, white or purple flowers. Several cultivars are available. Other popular campanulas include *C.* × '**Birch Hybrid**,' *C. glomerata* (clustered bellflower), *C. persicifolia* (peach-leaved bellflower) and *C. poscharskyana* (Serbian bellflower).

Features: blue, white, purple, spring, summer or fall flowers; varied growing habits **Height:** 4–36" **Spread:** 12–36" **Hardiness:** zones 3–7

Chrysanthemum

Chrysanthemum

Chrysanthemums are kings of the fall color parade. These botanical time bombs lie in wait all season, and then delight the senses with masses of bloom from September to frost.

Growing

Chrysanthemums grow best in **full sun**. The soil should be **fertile, moist** and **well drained**. Plant as early in the growing season as possible to increase the chances that plants will survive winter. Pinch plants back in early summer to encourage bushy growth and to increase flower production. Divide plants every two years to keep them growing vigorously.

Tips

Chrysanthemums provide a blaze of color in the fall garden that lasts until the first hard frost. Use them in groups or as specimen plants in borders and planters, or in plantings close to the house. When purchased in fall, they can be added to spots where summer annuals have faded.

Recommended

Many species, cultivars and hybrids are available. *C.* **Morden Series** plants are reliably hardy to zone 4, and come in a wide variety of colors. *C.* **Prophet Series** has cultivars with flowers in a wide range of colors.

C. hybrids (above & below)

You can deadhead in late fall or early winter, but leave the stems intact to protect the crowns of the plants.

Also called: fall garden mum **Features:** orange, yellow, pink, red, purple late-summer or fall flowers; habit **Height:** 10"–4' **Spread:** 18–36" **Hardiness:** zones 4–9

Coneflower
Echinacea

E. purpurea 'Magnus' and 'White Swan' (above), E. purpurea (below)

Coneflower attracts butterflies and other wildlife to the garden, providing pollen, nectar and seeds to the various hungry visitors.

The popularity of coneflowers is easy to understand. The large, daisy-like flowers can reach up to 6" across and are highly attractive to butterflies.

Growing
Coneflower grows well in **full sun** or very **light shade**. It tolerates any well-drained soil, but prefers an **average to rich** soil. The thick taproots make this plant drought resistant, but it prefers to have regular water. Divide it every four years or so in spring or fall.

Deadhead early in the season to prolong flowering. Later you may wish to leave the flowerheads in place to self-seed and provide winter interest. Pinch plants back or thin out the stems in early summer to encourage bushy growth that is less prone to mildew.

Tips
Use coneflowers in meadow gardens and informal borders, either in groups or as single specimens. The dry flowerheads make an interesting feature in fall and winter gardens.

Recommended
E. purpurea is an upright plant covered in prickly hairs. It bears purple flowers with orangy centers. Cultivars are available.

Also called: purple coneflower, echinacea
Features: purple, pink, white mid-summer to fall flowers with rusty orange centers; persistent seedheads **Height:** 2–5'
Spread: up to 18" **Hardiness:** zones 3–8

Euphorbia
Euphorbia

Euphorbia is not grown nearly enough by gardeners, except for (hint, hint) gardeners with really great-looking gardens.

Growing

Euphorbia grows well in **full sun** or **light shade,** in **moist, well-drained, humus-rich** soil of **average fertility.** This plant is drought tolerant and can be invasive and floppy in fertile soil. Euphorbia does not tolerate wet conditions. Plant it in spring or fall. Division is rarely required. Euphorbia dislikes being disturbed once established.

E. griffithii 'Fireglow' (above), E. polychroma (below)

Tips

Use euphorbia in a mixed or herbaceous border, rock garden or lightly shaded woodland garden.

Recommended

E. corollata (flowering spurge, tramp's spurge, wild spurge) is an erect plant with slender stems and a plethora of flowers with showy white bracts.

E. dulcis is compact and upright, bearing yellow-green bracts and dark bronze-green leaves that turn red and orange in fall. **'Chameleon'** has purple-red foliage that turns darker purple in fall.

E. griffithii **'Fireglow'** has light green leaves, orange stems and bright orange bracts.

E. polychroma (*E. epithimoides*) has inconspicuous flowers surrounded by long-lasting, yellow bracts. It has several cultivars.

You may wish to wear gloves when handling this plant because the sap contains latex, which can irritate the skin.

Also called: cushion spurge **Features:** colorful yellow, orange, white bracts in spring to mid-summer; fall foliage; low maintenance **Height:** 12–36" **Spread:** 12–24" **Hardiness:** zones 4–9

Foamflower

Tiarella

T. cordifolia (above & below)

Tiarella is a small genus of very useful shade plants grown both for their arresting flowers and their pleasing foliage. If a portion of your property contains woodlands, foamflowers are a natural to help in the transition.

Growing

Foamflowers prefer **partial light** or **full shade** without afternoon sun. The soil should be **humus rich, moist** and **slightly acidic,** though these plants adapt to most soils. Divide them in spring. Deadhead to encourage re-blooming. If the foliage fades or rusts in summer, cut it partway to the ground and new growth will emerge.

Tips

Foamflowers are excellent ground-covers for shaded and woodland gardens. They can be included in shaded borders and left to natural-ize in wild gardens.

Recommended

T. cordifolia is a low-growing, spreading plant that bears spikes of foamy-looking, white flowers. Cultivars are available. **'Oakleaf'** forms a dense clump of dark green leaves and bears pink flowers.

T. wherryi is similar to *T. cordifolia*, but it forms a clump and bears more flowers.

These plants spread by underground stems, which are easily pulled up to stop excessive spread.

Features: pink or white spring and, some-times, early-summer flowers; decorative foliage **Height:** 4–12" **Spread:** 12–24" **Hardiness:** zones 3–8

Goat's Beard
Aruncus

A. dioicus (above & below)

Aruncus is an outstanding North American native plant gaining popularity with each new season.

Growing

These plants prefer **partial to full shade**. In deep shade, they bear fewer blooms. They tolerate some full sun as long as the soil is kept evenly moist and they are protected from the afternoon sun. The soil should be **fertile, moist** and **humus rich**.

Divide in spring or fall. Use a sharp knife or an axe to cut the dense root mass into pieces. Fortunately, these plants rarely need dividing.

Tips

Goat's beard look very natural growing near the sunny entrance or edge of a woodland garden, in a native plant garden or in a large island planting. They may also be used in a border or alongside a stream or pond.

Recommended

A. aethusifolius (dwarf Korean goat's beard) forms a low-growing, compact mound and bears branched spikes of loosely held, cream flowers.

A. dioicus (giant goat's beard, common goat's beard) forms a large, bushy, shrub-like perennial with large plumes of creamy white flowers. There are several cultivars.

Male and female flowers are produced on separate plants. Male flowers are full and fuzzy whereas female flowers are more pendulous.

Features: cream or white early to mid-summer blooms; shrub-like habit; attractive foliage and seedheads
Height: 6"–6' **Spread:** 1–6' **Hardiness:** zones 3–7

Hardy Geranium

Geranium

G. sanguineum var. striatum (above), *G. sanguineum* (below)

Start growing hardy geraniums and your love for the plant will never wane. Intricate veining and patterns on both flowers and foliage keep this easy-to-grow perennial handsome before and after bloom.

Growing

Hardy geraniums grow well in **full sun**, **partial shade** or **light shade** in **well-drained** soil of **average fertility**. These plants dislike hot weather. Divide in spring. Shear back spent blooms for a second set of flowers.

If the foliage looks tatty in late summer, prune it back to rejuvenate it.

Tips

These long-flowering plants are great in a border. They fill in space between shrubs and other larger plants, and they keep the weeds down. Hardy geraniums can also be included in rock gardens and woodland gardens, or mass planted as groundcovers.

Recommended

There is an abundance of excellent species, cultivars and hybrids that do well in our two states. Most are mound-forming plants. Some produce a basal rosette of foliage and some form mats of creeping foliage. *G. sanguineum* (bloody cranesbill, bloodred cranesbill) is the most common, but check with your local garden center or nursery to see what is available.

Also called: cranesbill geranium
Features: white, red, pink, purple, blue summer flowers; attractive, sometimes fragrant foliage **Height:** 2–36"
Spread: 12–36" **Hardiness:** zones 3–8

Heuchera

Heuchera

$\mathcal{F}$ew perennials available to northern gardeners offer the tremendous variety of foliage sizes, shapes and colors as heuchera.

Growing

Heucheras grow best in **light or partial shade**. The foliage colors can bleach out in full sun, and plants grow leggy in full shade. The soil should be of **average to rich fertility, humus rich, neutral to alkaline, moist** and **well drained**. Good air circulation is essential.

Deadhead to prolong the bloom. Every two or three years, heucheras should be dug up and the oldest, woodiest roots and stems removed. Plants may be divided at this time, and then replanted with the crown at or just above soil level.

H. × brizioides 'Firefly' (above), H. sanguineum (below)

Tips

Use heucheras as edging plants, in woodland gardens or as groundcovers in low-traffic areas. Combine different foliage types for an interesting display.

Heucheras have a strange habit of pushing themselves up out of the soil. Mulch in fall if the plants begin heaving from the ground.

Recommended

There are dozens of beautiful cultivars available with almost limitless variations of foliage markings and colors. See your local garden center or mail-order catalog to see what is available.

Also called: coral bells, alum root
Features: very decorative foliage; red, pink, white, yellow, purple spring or summer flowers **Height:** 6"–4'
Spread: 12–18" **Hardiness:** zones 3–9

Hosta

Hosta

H. fortunei 'Francee' (above)

Some gardeners think the flowers clash with the foliage, and they remove the flower stems when they first emerge. If you find the flowers unattractive, removing them won't harm the plant.

Entering the world of hostas can be intimidating. Our advice is to cover the basics: start out by purchasing a blue, a gold, a green, and a variegated hosta.

Growing

Hostas prefer **light or partial shade** but will grow in full shade. Morning sun is preferable to afternoon sun. The soil should ideally be **fertile, moist** and **well drained**, but most soils are tolerated. Hostas are fairly drought tolerant, especially if using mulch. Division is not required but can be done every few years in spring or summer to propagate new plants.

Tips

Hostas make wonderful woodland plants and look great when combined with ferns and other fine-textured plants. Hostas work well in mixed borders, particularly when used to hide the leggy lower stems and branches of some shrubs. Hostas' dense growth and thick, shade-providing leaves help to suppress weeds.

Recommended

There are hundreds of hosta species, cultivars and hybrids. Visit your local garden center or get a mail-order catalog to find out what's available.

Also called: plantain lily **Features:** decorative foliage; white or purple summer and fall flowers **Height:** 4"–6' **Spread:** 16"–6' **Hardiness:** zones 3–8

Iris

Iris

*O*ris is one of the great marvels of the garden. The sharp, vertical slash of iris foliage is an essential component of garden design.

Growing

Irises prefer **full sun** but tolerate very light or dappled shade. The soil should be of **average fertility** and **well drained**. Japanese and Siberian iris prefer a moist, well-drained soil. Deadhead irises to keep them tidy. Cut back the foliage of Siberian iris in spring.

Divide in late summer or early fall. Replant bearded iris rhizomes with the flat side of the foliage fan facing the garden. Dust the rhizome with a powder cleanser before planting to help prevent soft rot.

Tips

Irises are popular border plants. Japanese and Siberian iris grow well alongside streams or ponds. Dwarf cultivars look attractive in rock gardens.

I. sibirica (above), *I. germanica* 'Stepping Out' (below)

Irises can cause severe internal irritation if ingested. Always wash your hands after handling them. Avoid planting irises where children play.

Recommended

Many species and hybrids are available. Among the most popular is bearded iris, often a hybrid of *I. germanica*. It has the widest range of flower colors but is susceptible to iris borer. Several irises are not susceptible, including Japanese iris (*I. ensata*) and Siberian iris (*I. sibirica*).

Features: spring, summer and sometimes fall flowers in many shades of pink, red, purple, blue, white, brown, yellow; attractive foliage
Height: 6"–4' **Spread:** 6"–4'
Hardiness: zones 3–10

Joe-Pye Weed
Eupatorium

E. rugosum (above), E. maculatum (below)

Growing

Joe-Pye weed prefers **full sun** but tolerates partial shade. The soil should be **fertile** and **moist**. Wet soils are tolerated. Divide plants in spring when clumps become overgrown.

Pruning growth back in May encourages branching and lower, denser growth, but it can delay flowering. It may take a couple of seasons for these plants to mature, so don't crowd them.

Tips

The tall types are ideal in the back of a border or center of a bed where they will create a backdrop for lower-growing plants.

If you want a bold, beautiful perennial, here's your chance. Joe-Pye looks great around lakes and ponds, at the back of borders, and mixed in with tall grasses and prairie plants.

Recommended

E. maculatum is a huge plant that bears clusters of purple flowers.

E. perfoliatum (common boneset, thoroughwort) is a clump-forming plant bearing large clusters of purple-tinged, white flowers.

E. purpureum (sweet Joe Pye weed) is a large, clump-forming plant with purple-tinged stems, large, purple-tinged, midgreen foliage and domed clusters of pink to purple-pink flowers.

E. rugosum (*Ageratina altissima*; boneset, white snakeroot) forms a bushy, mounding clump bearing white flowers.

Also called: boneset, snakeroot **Features:** attractive foliage; white, purple, blue, pink late summer and fall flowers **Height:** 2–9' **Spread:** 2–4' **Hardiness:** zones 3–9

Lady's Mantle
Alchemilla

*A*lchemilla is a complete plant, meaning that the flower color and form, and foliage color and form contrast so beautifully with each other that the plant is an utter spectacle in and of itself.

Growing
Lady's mantle plants prefer **light or partial shade**, with protection from the afternoon sun. They dislike hot locations, and excessive sun will scorch their leaves. The soil should be **fertile, humus rich, moist** and **well drained**. These plants are drought resistant once established.

The leaves can be sheared back in summer if they begin to look tired and heat-stressed. Deadhead to keep plants looking tidy and to prevent excessive reseeding. Division is rarely required.

Tips
Lady's mantles are ideal in woodland gardens and along border edges, where they soften the bright colors of other plants. They are also attractive in containers.

A. mollis (above & below)

The young leaves of these plants have a mildly bitter flavor and can be added to salads and dips.

Recommended
A. erythropoda is a clump-forming plant with dense, blue-green to gray foliage and stems that turn red in the sun.

A. mollis (common Lady's mantle) is the most common of the species. It forms a mound of soft, rounded foliage, above which are held sprays of frothy-looking, yellowish green flowers.

Features: yellow to chartreuse early-summer to early-fall flowers; attractive foliage; habit
Height: 6–18" **Spread:** 8–24"
Hardiness: zones 3–7

Lamium

Lamium

L. maculatum 'White Nancy' (above), *L. maculatum* 'Beacon Silver' (below)

*L*amium is a splendid shade groundcover we consider an essential perennial for northern gardeners. In flower it is wonderful, but the key to its value is its weaving mounds of fabulously attractive, variegated foliage.

Growing

Lamiums prefer **partial to light shade** in **humus-rich, moist, well-drained** soil of **average fertility**. These plants grow vigorously in fertile soil. They are drought tolerant in the shade, but can develop bare patches if the soil is allowed to dry out for extended periods. Divide and replant in fall if bare spots become unsightly.

Plants remain compact if sheared back after flowering. If they remain green over the winter, shear back in early spring.

Tips

These plants make useful groundcovers for woodland or shade gardens. They work well under shrubs in a border, where they help keep weeds down.

Recommended

L. galeobdolon (*Lamiastrum galeobdolon*; yellow archangel) has yellow flowers and can be quite invasive, though the cultivars are less so.

L. maculatum (spotted dead nettle) is a low-growing, spreading species with green leaves marked with white or silver. It bears white, pink or mauve flowers. Many cultivars are available.

Also called: dead nettle **Features:** white, pink, yellow, mauve spring or summer flowers; decorative, often-variegated foliage **Height:** 8–24" **Spread:** indefinite **Hardiness:** zones 3–8

Liatris
Liatris

Liatris stems shoot up from the ground, producing dense, bushy spikes of pinkish purple or white flowers. Clumps of liatris are bee and butterfly magnets, and they are always dazzling additions to sunny hot spots.

Growing

Liatris prefers **full sun**. The soil should be of **average fertility, sandy, well drained** and **humus rich**. Water well during the growing season, but don't allow the plants to stand in water during cool weather. Mulch during summer to prevent moisture loss.

Trim off the spent flower spikes to promote a longer blooming period and to keep liatris looking tidy. Divide every three or four years in fall. The clump will appear crowded when it is time to divide.

Tips

Use liatris in borders and meadow plantings. Plant it in a location that has good drainage to avoid root rot in winter. Liatris also does well in planters.

Recommended

L. spicata is a clump-forming, erect plant. Several cultivars are available. Other good liatris species include *L. aspera* (rough gayfeather, royal blazing star), *L. punctata* (snakeroot) and *L. pycnostachya* (button snakeroot, Kansas gayfeather, prairie blazing star).

L. spicata 'Kobold' (above), L. spicata (below)

Forget color for a moment—the supreme value of liatris is the vertical element and contrast in form it brings to any planting.

Also called: blazing star, spike gayfeather, gayfeather **Features:** purple or white summer flowers; grass-like foliage **Height:** 18"–6' **Spread:** 18–24" **Hardiness:** zones 3–9

Ligularia
Ligularia

L. stenocephala 'The Rocket' (above), L. dentata (below)

Growing
Ligularias should be grown in **light shade** or **partial shade** with protection from the afternoon sun. The soil should be of **average fertility, humus rich** and **consistently moist**. The foliage can wilt in hot sun, even in moist soil. The leaves will revive overnight, but it is best to plant ligularia in a cool, shaded place.

Division is rarely required but can be done in spring or fall.

Tips
Plant ligularias alongside a pond or stream. They can also be used in a well-watered border or bog garden, or naturalized in a moist meadow or woodland garden.

igularia makes our list of complete plants; that is, one with a flowering habit that contrasts splendidly with its foliage.

Recommended
L. dentata (bigleaf ligularia, golden groundsel) forms a clump of rounded, heart-shaped leaves and bears clusters of orange-yellow, daisy-like flowers. Cultivars are available in varied sizes and colors.

L. przewalskii (Shevalski's ligularia) forms a clump of deeply incised leaves. It produces yellow flowers on long, purple spikes.

L. stenocephala (narrow-spiked ligularia) has toothed foliage and bears bright yellow flowers on dark purple-green spikes. 'The Rocket' has heart-shaped leaves with ragged-toothed margins and dark leaf veins.

Features: yellow or orange summer to early fall flowers; ornate foliage **Height:** 3–6' **Spread:** 2–5' **Hardiness:** zones 4–8

Meadowsweet

Filipendula

The charms of meadow-sweet extend from the formal garden to meadow plantings, cottage gardens and pondside placements. It has proved itself reliable in even the northernmost stretches of Wisconsin and Minnesota.

Growing

Meadowsweets prefer **partial or light shade**, but tolerate full sun if the soil remains sufficiently moist. The soil should be **fertile, deep, humus rich** and **moist**, except in the case of *F. vulgaris*, which prefers dry soil. Divide in spring or fall.

Tips

Most meadowsweets are excellent plants for wet sites such as bog gardens, alongside streams or moist meadows. They can be grown in beds and borders, as long as they are kept well watered. Grow *F. vulgaris* if you can't provide the moisture needed by the other species.

F. rubra (above), F. ulmaria (below)

The faded seedheads are quite attractive when left in place.

Recommended

Cultivars of each species are available.

F. rubra (queen-of-the-prairie) forms a large, spreading clump and bears clusters of fragrant, pink flowers.

F. ulmaria (queen-of-the-meadow) forms a mounding clump and bears creamy white flowers in large clusters.

F. vulgaris (dropwort, meadowsweet) is a low-growing species that bears clusters of fragrant, creamy white flowers.

Features: white, cream, pink, red late-spring or summer flowers; attractive foliage **Height:** 2–8' **Spread:** 18"–4'
Hardiness: zones 3–8

Obedient Plant

Physostegia

P. virginiana (above & below)

Growing

Obedient plants prefer **full sun** but tolerate partial or light shade. The soil should be **moist** and of **average to high fertility**. In a fertile soil these plants are more vigorous and may need staking. Compact cultivars rarely need staking. Plants can become invasive. Divide in early to mid-spring, every two years or so to curtail invasiveness. Floppy plants can be pruned or pinched by one-half in spring for slightly shorter, sturdier growth.

Tips

Use these plants in borders, cottage gardens, informal borders and naturalistic gardens. The flowers of obedient plants can be cut for use in fresh arrangements.

Recommended

P. virginiana has upright stems and a spreading root system. **'Bouquet Rose'** bears lilac-pink flowers. **'Summer Snow'** is a more compact, less invasive plant with white flowers. **'Variegata'** is a desirable variegated specimen with cream-margined leaves and bright pink flowers.

P. **'Vivid'** is a compact hybrid that bears bright purple-pink flowers.

Features: pink, purple, white mid-summer to fall flowers
Height: 1–4' **Spread:** 12–24"
Hardiness: zones 2–9

extremely easy to grow and hardy to the most northern extremes, *Physostegia* looks great massed in waves in a large garden.

The individual flowers can be bent around on the stems and will stay put where you place them. It is this unusual habit that gives the plant its common name.

Ox-eye
Heliopsis

H. helianthoides (above & below)

If only northern gardeners could grow a bushy, free-flowing perennial featuring big, bountiful, bright yellow blooms that lasted for a good part of summer, was virtually pest- and disease-free, didn't care much about soil, and would thrive in sun to light shade. Hey, wait a minute, we can!

Growing

Ox-eye prefers **full sun** but tolerates partial shade. The soil should be **average to fertile, humus rich, moist** and **well drained**. Most soil conditions are tolerated, including poor, dry soils. Divide every two years or so.

Deadhead to prolong the blooming period. Cut plants back once flowering is complete if appearance is tatty. Allow a few seedheads to remain, as these short-lived plants are reliable self-seeders, and the finches love them.

Tips

Use ox-eye at the back or in the middle of mixed or herbaceous borders. Combine it with coneflowers, mid-season blooming asters and liatris to attract butterflies and bees to your garden.

Recommended

H. helianthoides forms an upright clump of stems and foliage and bears yellow or orange, daisy-like flowers. 'Ballerina' grows 36" tall and has single, golden yellow flowers. 'Incomparabilis' has double, bright golden yellow flowers. 'Summer Sun' ('Sommersonne') bears single or semi-double flowers in bright golden yellow. It grows about 36" tall.

Also called: false sunflower, orange sunflower
Features: yellow and orange, mid-summer to mid-fall flowers; attractive foliage; easy to grow
Height: 3–5' **Spread:** 18–36" **Hardiness:** zones 2–9

Peony

Paeonia

P. lactiflora cultivars (above & below)

Growing

Peonies prefer **full sun** but tolerate some shade. Peonies like **fertile, humus-rich, moist, well-drained** soil with a lot of compost. Prepare the soil before planting. Mulch peonies lightly with compost in spring. Too much fertilizer, particularly nitrogen, causes floppy growth and retards blooming. Divide in fall to propagate plants. Deadhead to keep plants looking tidy. Clean up around peonies in fall to reduce the possibility of disease.

Tips

Peonies look great in a border combined with other early bloomers. Avoid planting peonies where they have to compete for moisture and nutrients.

Tubers planted too shallow or, more commonly, too deep, will not flower. The buds or eyes on the tuber should be 1–2" below the soil surface.

Peonies are one of the longest-lived perennials. They are easy to grow, tough as nails and add backbone to the garden that few other perennials can match.

Place wire tomato or peony cages around the plants in early spring to support the heavy flowers. The growing foliage will hide the cage.

Recommended

There are hundreds of peonies. Cultivars come in a wide range of colors, bearing single or double flowers, and may or may not be fragrant. Visit your local garden center to see what is available.

Features: white, cream, yellow, pink, red, purple spring and early-summer flowers; attractive foliage **Height:** 24–36" **Spread:** 24–36" **Hardiness:** zones 2–7

Phlox
Phlox

Phlox comprises a widely diverse group of beautiful plants for sun to partial shade.

Growing

Garden phlox and early phlox prefer **full sun**. Moss phlox prefers **partial shade**. Creeping phlox prefers **light to partial shade** but tolerates heavy shade. All like **fertile, humus-rich, moist, well-drained** soil. Divide in fall or spring.

Do not prune creeping phlox in fall—it will have next spring's flowers already forming.

Tips

Low-growing species are useful in a rock garden or at the front of a border. Taller species may be used in the middle of a border, particularly when planted in groups.

Garden phlox requires good air circulation to help prevent mildew. Thin out large stands to help keep the air flowing. Early phlox is more mildew resistant.

P. subulata (above), *P. paniculata* cultivar (below)

Recommended

P. maculata (Maculata Group; early phlox, wild sweet William) forms an upright clump of hairy stems and pink, purple or white flowers.

P. paniculata (Paniculata Group; garden phlox) blooms in summer and fall. It has many cultivars in a variety of sizes and flower colors.

P. stolonifera (creeping phlox) is a low, spreading plant with purple flowers. It grows roots where the stems touch the ground.

P. subulata (moss phlox, creeping phlox, moss pinks) is very low growing.

Features: white, orange, red, blue, purple, pink spring, summer or fall flowers; plant habit **Height:** 2"–4'
Spread: 12–36" **Hardiness:** zones 3–8

Russian Sage

Perovskia

P. atriplicifolia (above), *P. atriplicifolia* 'Filigran' (below)

*A*ttractive all season, glorious in bloom, Russian sage is an easy-to-grow, long-lived perennial possessing a lengthy bloom period across late summer.

Growing

Russian sage prefers **full sun**. The soil should be **poor to moderately fertile** and **well drained**. Too much water and nitrogen will cause this plant to flop, so do not plant it next to heavy feeders. Russian sage cannot be divided because it is a subshrub that originates from a single stem.

In spring, when new growth appears low on the branches, or in fall, cut the plant back hard to about 6–12" to encourage vigorous, bushy growth.

Russian sage blossoms make a lovely addition to fresh bouquets and dried-flower arrangements.

Tips

The silvery foliage and blue flowers soften the appearance of daylilies and work well with other plants in the back of a mixed border. Russian sage can also create a soft screen in a natural garden or on a dry bank.

Recommended

P. atriplicifolia is a loose, upright plant with silvery white, finely divided foliage. The small, lavender blue flowers are loosely held on silvery, branched stems. '**Filigran**' has delicate foliage and an upright habit. '**Longin**' is narrow and erect.

Features: blue or purple mid-summer to autumn flowers; attractive habit; fragrant, gray-green foliage **Height:** 3–4'
Spread: 3–4'
Hardiness: zones 4–9

Sedum
Sedum

Some gardeners aren't aware of just how huge and useful this diverse family of plants is. Sedums feature outstanding foliage that complements surrounding plants throughout the season.

Growing

Sedums prefer **full sun** but tolerate partial shade. The soil should be of **average fertility, very well drained** and **neutral to alkaline.** Divide in spring when needed.

Tips

Low-growing sedums make wonderful groundcovers and additions to rock gardens or rock walls. They edge beds and borders beautifully. Taller sedums give a lovely late-season display in a bed or border.

Recommended

There are 300 to 500 species of sedum throughout the Northern Hemisphere, including the following popular selections.

S. acre (gold moss stonecrop) is a low-growing, wide-spreading plant that bears small, yellow-green flowers.

S. 'Autumn Joy' (*Hylotelephium* 'Autumn Joy'; autumn joy sedum) is an upright hybrid with flowers that open pink or red and later fade to deep bronze.

S. 'Autumn Joy' (above & below)

S. spectabile (showy stonecrop) is an upright species with pink flowers. Cultivars are available.

S. spurium (two-row stonecrop) forms a low, wide mat of foliage with deep pink or white flowers. Cultivars are available bearing colorful foliage.

Also called: stonecrop Features: yellow, white, red, pink summer to fall flowers; decorative, fleshy foliage; easy to grow Height: 2–30" Spread: 12" to indefinite Hardiness: zones 3–9

Speedwell
Veronica

V. 'Sunny Border Blue' (above), *V. spicata* 'Red Fox' (below)

Veronica is an excellent, long-lived perennial for new gardeners to start with.

Growing
Speedwells prefer **full sun** but tolerate partial shade. The soil should be of **average fertility, moist** and **well drained**. Lack of sun and excessive moisture and nitrogen may be partly to blame for the sloppy habits of some speedwells. Divide in fall or spring every two or three years to ensure strong, vigorous growth and to decrease the chances of flopping.

When the flowers begin to fade, remove the entire spike where it joins the plant to encourage rapid re-blooming. For tidy plants, shear back to 6" in June.

Tips
Low-growing speedwells are useful in a rock garden or at the front of a perennial border. Upright speedwells work well in masses in a bed or border.

Recommended
Wonderful cultivars and hybrids, such as *V.* **'Goodness Grows,'** are available. Check with your local garden center to see what is available.

V. prostrata (prostrate speedwell) is a low-growing, spreading plant with blue, or occasionally, pink flowers.

V. spicata (spike speedwell) is a low, mounding plant with stems that flop over when they get too tall. It bears spikes of blue flowers.

Also called: veronica **Features:** white, pink, purple or blue summer flowers; varied habits **Height:** 3–30" **Spread:** 3–18" **Hardiness:** zones 3–8

Yarrow
Achillea

A. millefolium 'Paprika' (above), *A. filipendulina* (below)

arrows are exceptional perennials, and a sunny garden is where they should be found.

Growing

Grow yarrows in **full sun** in **well-drained** soil of **average fertility**. These plants tolerate drought and poor soil, and abide, but do not thrive in, heavy, wet soil or very humid conditions. Excessively rich soil or too much nitrogen results in weak, floppy growth. Staking may be needed. Divide every two or three years in spring.

Deadhead to prolong blooming. The basal foliage should be left in place over the winter and tidied up in spring.

Tips

Cottage gardens, wildflower gardens and mixed borders are perfect places for these informal plants. They thrive in hot, dry locations where nothing else will grow.

Recommended

A. filipendulina forms a clump of ferny foliage and bears yellow flowers. It has been used to develop several hybrids and cultivars.

A. millefolium (common yarrow) forms a clump of soft, finely divided foliage and bears white flowers. Many cultivars exist with flowers in many colors.

Yarrows make excellent groundcovers. They send up shoots and flowers from a low basal point and may be mowed periodically without excessive damage to the plant. Mower blades should be kept at least 4" high.

Features: white, yellow, red, orange, pink, purple mid-summer to early fall flowers; attractive foliage; spreading habit
Height: 12"–5' **Spread:** 12–36" **Hardiness:** zones 3–9

Arborvitae
Thuja

T. occidentalis 'Yellow Ribbon' (above), *T. occidentalis* (below)

Many diverse cultivars of T. occidentalis *are available, from pyramidal forms that make excellent specimens, and yellow types that add color to the winter landscape, to dwarf, globe-shaped forms for the mixed border or rock garden.*

*F*ew evergreen shrubs offer such wide variety in height, growth, habit and coloration as *Thuja*. Once established, these plants suffer little winterburn, which makes this genus ideal for our region.

Growing
Arborvitae prefer **full sun,** although some varieties grow reasonably well in partial shade. The soil should be of **average fertility, moist** and **well drained**. These plants enjoy humidity and are often found growing near marshy areas. Arborvitae perform best in locations with some **shelter** from the wind, especially in winter, when the foliage can easily dry out.

These plants take very well to pruning and are often grown as hedges. They may be kept formally shaped, or clipped to maintain a loose but compact shape and size.

Tips
Large varieties of arborvitae make excellent specimen trees, and smaller cultivars can be used in foundation plantings and shrub borders, and as formal or informal hedges.

Recommended
T. occidentalis (eastern arborvitae, eastern white cedar) is a narrow pyramidal tree with scale-like needles. The species is hardy to zone 2; cultivars may be less cold hardy.

Also called: cedar **Features:** small to large evergreen shrub or tree; foliage; bark; form **Height:** 1–30' **Spread:** 1–15' **Hardiness:** zones 2–8

Barberry
Berberis

The great joy of landscaping with shrubs is in the exploration of the seemingly endless variations in foliage form, texture and color. Few shrub families reward this examination as generously as barberries.

Growing

Barberry develops the best fall color when grown in **full sun**, but it tolerates partial shade. Any **well-drained** soil is suitable. This plant tolerates drought and urban conditions but suffers in poorly drained, wet soil.

Tips

Large barberry plants make great hedges with formidable prickles. Barberry can also be included in shrub and mixed borders. Small cultivars can be grown in rock gardens, in raised beds and along rock walls.

Recommended

B. 'Bailsel' (GOLDEN CAROUSEL) is an upright shrub with arching branches. The new foliage emerges golden yellow. Fall color is orange to red. The fruit is bright red.

B. × 'Tara' (EMERALD CAROUSEL) is a rounded shrub with arching branches. The dark green foliage turns reddish purple in fall. The showy fruit is bright red.

B. thunbergii 'Aurea' (above), *B. thunbergii* 'Atropurpurea' (below)

B. thunbergii (Japanese barberry) is a dense, broad, rounded shrub with bright green foliage that turns shades of orange, red or purple in fall. Yellow flowers are followed by glossy red fruit. Many cultivars have been developed for their foliage color, including shades of purple, yellow and variegated varieties.

Features: prickly, deciduous shrub; foliage; yellow spring flowers; fruit **Height:** 1–6' **Spread:** 18"–6' **Hardiness:** zones 4–8

Beech

Fagus

F. sylvatica 'Purpurea Pendula' (above), *F. sylvatica* (below)

Beeches are magnificent trees, particularly when the homeowner respects these plants' desire to grow their densely foliated branches nearly to the ground.

Growing

Beeches grow equally well in **full sun** or **partial shade**. The soil should be of **average fertility, loamy** and **well drained**, though almost all well-drained soils are tolerated.

American beech suffers in alkaline and poorly drained soils. It also doesn't like having its roots disturbed and should be transplanted only when very young. European beech transplants easily and is more tolerant of varied soil conditions than is American beech.

The nuts are edible when roasted.

Tips

Beeches make excellent specimens. They are also used as shade trees and in woodland gardens. These trees need a lot of space, but the European beech's adaptability to pruning makes it a reasonable choice in a small garden.

Recommended

F. grandifolia (American beech) is a broad-canopied tree native to most of eastern North America.

F. sylvatica (European beech) is a spectacular broad tree with a number of interesting cultivars. Several are small enough to use in the home garden, from narrow columnar and weeping varieties to those with purple or yellow leaves, or pink, white and green variegated foliage.

Features: large, oval, deciduous shade tree; foliage; bark; fall color; fruit
Height: 30–80' **Spread:** 10–60'
Hardiness: zones 4–9

Birch
Betula

or four-season interest (never forget that we have long winters up here!), there isn't a more important small to mid-sized deciduous tree to plant, grow and enjoy than birch.

Growing
Birches grow well in **full sun, partial shade** or **light shade**. The soil should be of **average to high fertility, moist** and fairly **well drained**. Periodic flooding is tolerated but persistently wet soils will kill these trees. Provide supplemental water to all birches during periods of extended drought.

Tips
Birch trees are often used as specimens. Their small leaves and open canopy provide light shade that allows perennials, annuals and lawns to flourish underneath. Birches look attractive when grown in groups near natural or artificial water features.

Recommended
The following species all resist bronze birch borer attacks.

B. nigra (river birch, black birch, red birch) has shaggy, cinnamon brown bark that flakes off in sheets, then thickens and becomes more ridged as the tree matures. 'Little King' (FOX VALLEY) is a dwarf cultivar with a broad, pyramidal habit. (Zones 3–9)

B. nigra (above & below)

B. papyrifera 'Renci' (RENAISSANCE REFLECTIONS) is a fast-growing, heat-tolerant, pyramidal, single- or multi-stemmed tree. (Zones 2–7)

B. szechuanica 'Royal Frost' is a smaller clump variety with rich burgundy foliage, bronze-tinged exfoliating bark and brilliant fall color ranging from yellow-orange to red. (Zones 4–9)

Features: open, deciduous tree; attractive foliage; bark; fall color; winter and spring catkins **Height:** 10–90' **Spread:** 10–60' **Hardiness:** zones 2–9

Boxwood

Buxus

B. microphylla var. *koreana* × *B. sempervirens* hybrid (above & below)

American landscape design has slowly loosed itself from English gardening traditions, and boxwoods are being planted with new appreciation…and without hard shearing and shaping!

Growing

Boxwoods prefer **partial shade** but adapt to full shade or to full sun if kept well watered. The soil should be **fertile** and **well drained**. Once established, boxwoods are drought tolerant.

Using mulch will benefit these shrubs because of their shallow roots. Do not disturb the earth around a boxwood once it is established.

Tips

Boxwoods are often used to form dense evergreen hedges. These shrubs make excellent background plants in mixed borders. Boxwood topiary can create a formal or whimsical focal point in any garden.

Recommended

B. microphylla var. *koreana* (Korean littleleaf boxwood) is cold hardy and quite pest resistant. The foliage turns shades of bronze, yellow or brown in winter.

Cultivars developed from crossing *B. m.* var. *koreana* and *B. sempervirens* exhibit good hardiness and pest resistance, and have attractive year-round foliage.

B. sinica insularis 'Wintergreen' (*B. microphylla* var. *koreana* 'Winter Green') is a dense, mounding shrub that keeps its light green foliage color through the winter.

B. 'Wilson' (NORTHERN CHARM) is a cold-hardy, compact, oval shrub that has semi-glossy, emerald green foliage with a bluish cast.

Features: foliage; slow, even growth; dense, rounded, evergreen shrub **Height:** 2–8' **Spread:** equal to or slightly greater than height **Hardiness:** zones 4–8

Cherry, Plum & Almond

Prunus

Compact sizes, wonderful forms, breathtaking spring blooms and vivid fall colors make these trees and shrubs worth much consideration.

Growing

These plants prefer **full sun** and **moist, well-drained** soil of **average fertility**. Plant them on mounds when possible to encourage drainage. Shallow roots will come up from the ground if the tree isn't getting enough water.

Tips

Prunus trees and shrubs make beautiful specimens. Many are small enough to include in almost any garden. Use small species and cultivars in borders or group them to form informal hedges or barriers.

P. tomentosa (above)

Cherries can be short-lived. If you plant a pest-susceptible species, such as *P. serrulata*, enjoy it while it thrives, but be prepared to replace it once problems surface. Pest-resistant species include *P. sargentii* and *P. subhirtella*.

Recommended

There are many wonderful *Prunus* species, hybrids and cultivars available. Check with your local nursery or garden center to see what is available.

The fruits, though not the pits, of Prunus *species are edible, but ornamental selections are not very tasty. Eating too much of the often-sour fruit can cause stomachaches.*

Features: upright, rounded, spreading or weeping deciduous tree or shrub; attractive, pink or white spring to early-summer flowers; fruit; bark; fall foliage **Height:** 3–75' **Spread:** 3–50' **Hardiness:** zones 2–9

Chokeberry

Aronia

A. melanocarpa (left), *A. melanocarpa* 'Autumn Magic' (right), *A. melanocarpa* (below)

Chokeberries are handsome, tough, easy-to-grow shrubs that bear lovely, fragrant white flowers, attractive, shiny, dark green foliage, great fall color and persistent, showy fruit.

Growing

Chokeberry grows well in full sun or partial shade, but the best flowering and fruiting occur in **full sun**. It grows best in **well-drained** soil of **average fertility** but adapts to most soils and generally tolerates wet, dry or poor soil. 'Brilliantissima' prefers moist to wet soil.

Up to one-third of the stems, preferably the older ones, can be pruned out annually once flowering has finished.

Tips

Chokeberry is useful in a shrub or mixed border. It also makes an interesting low-maintenance specimen. Left to its own devices, it will colonize a fairly large area.

Recommended

A. arbutifolia (*Photinia floribunda*; red chokeberry) is an upright shrub bearing bright red, waxy fruit and orange-red fall foliage. '**Brilliantissima**' has brilliant red fall foliage.

A. melanocarpa (black chokeberry) is an upright, suckering shrub. It bears dark fruit that ripens in fall and persists through winter. The foliage turns bright red to purplish red in fall.

Chokeberry fruit is high in vitamins, especially vitamin C. It is used as an easily available alternative to citrus in parts of Russia.

Features: suckering, deciduous shrub; white flowers; fruit; fall foliage **Height:** 3–8' **Spread:** 3–8' **Hardiness:** zones 3–8

Coralberry

Symphoricarpos

Coralberry is a native shrub deserving of much greater popularity than currently surrounds the plant.

Growing

Coralberries grow well in **full sun, partial or light shade** in any soil that is **fertile** and **well drained**. These plants can handle pollution, drought and exposure.

Tips

Use in shrub or mixed borders, in woodland gardens or as screens or informal hedges. On hillsides their suckering roots bind the soil.

Recommended

S. albus (common snowberry) is a rounded, suckering native shrub with arching branches, small, delicate pinkish white flowers and white berries. It tolerates clay soil. (Zones 3–7)

S. albus (above & below)

S. × chenaultii (Chenault coralberry) is an erect, well-branched shrub that spreads by suckers. It bears greenish white flowers and pink-tinged or pink-spotted, white fruit. (Zones 4–7)

S. × doorenbosii is a vigorous, thicket-forming hybrid that spreads indefinitely from suckers. It bears pink-tinged, greenish white flowers and pink-tinged, white fruit. Cultivars are available. (Zones 4–7)

S. orbiculatus (coralberry, Indian currant) is a dense, well-branched, erect to arching shrub. It has pink-tinged, yellowish white flowers and small, bright red-pink to dark red-purple fruit.

The berries are not edible and should be left for the birds.

Also called: snowberry **Features:** rounded or spreading deciduous shrub; dark green foliage; fall and winter fruit; white, or white tinged with pink, green, yellow summer flowers **Height:** 1–6' **Spread:** 3–12' **Hardiness:** zones 2–7

Crabapple
Malus

M. floribunda 'Snowdrift' (above)

Of all the ornamental trees, crabapples are the most popular with northern gardeners.

Growing

Crabapples prefer **full sun** but tolerate partial shade. The soil should be of **average to rich fertility, moist** and **well drained.** These trees tolerate damp soil.

One of the best ways to prevent the spread of crabapple pests and diseases is to clean up all the leaves and fruit that fall off the tree. Many pests overwinter in the fruit, leaves or soil at the base of the tree. Clearing away the pests' winter shelter helps keep their population under control.

Tips

Crabapples make excellent specimen plants. Many varieties are quite small, so there is one to suit almost any size of garden, and some are even small enough to grow in large containers. Crabapples are good choices for creating espalier specimens along a wall or fence.

Recommended

There are hundreds of crabapples available. When choosing a species, variety or cultivar, look for disease resistance. Even the most beautiful plant will never look good if ravaged by pests or diseases. Ask for information about new resistant cultivars at your local nursery or garden center. Always choose plants that are appropriate to the hardiness zone.

Features: rounded, mounded or spreading, small to medium, deciduous tree; pink, red, white spring flowers; late-season and winter fruit; fall foliage; bark
Height: 6–35' **Spread:** 5–30' **Hardiness:** zones 2–8

Dogwood
Cornus

C. alba 'Bailhalo' (above), *C. kousa* var. *chinensis* (below)

$\mathcal{W}$hether your garden is wet, dry, sunny or shaded, there is a dogwood for almost every condition. Stem color, leaf variegation, fall color, growth habit, soil adaptability and hardiness are all positive attributes to be found in the dogwoods.

Growing
Tree dogwoods grow well in **light shade** or **partial shade**. Shrub dogwoods prefer full sun or partial shade, with the best stem colors developing in **full sun**. The soil should be of **average to high fertility, high in organic matter, neutral or slightly acidic** and **well drained.** Shrub dogwoods prefer moist soil. *C. sericea* tolerates wet soil.

Tips
Use shrub dogwoods in a shrub or mixed border. They look best planted in groups. The tree species make wonderful specimen plants and are small enough to include in most gardens.

Recommended
Small shrub species and their cultivars are tough plants, often grown for their bright red, orange or yellow stems that provide winter interest. The larger shrubs and trees bear inconspicuous flowers surrounded by showy white or pink bracts in spring or early summer. Some species have attractive horizontal branching and some bear showy fruit. Many have attractive fall color. Check with your local garden center for availability and species appropriate to your hardiness zone.

Features: deciduous shrub or small tree; white or pink late-spring to early-summer flower bracts; fall foliage; stem color; fruit **Height:** 5–30' **Spread:** 5–30' **Hardiness:** zones 2–9

Elderberry
Sambucus

S. canadensis (above), *S. racemosa* (below)

*D*ismiss the notion that elderberries are weedy, common natives besmirching roadsides and abandoned clearings. Elderberries are fantastic ornamental shrubs, and the newer varieties are proving very popular with homeowners across North America.

Growing

Elderberries grow well in **full sun** or **partial shade** in **moist, well-drained** soil of **average fertility**. Cultivars grown for burgundy or black leaf color develop the best color in full sun, while cultivars with yellow leaf color develop the best color in light or partial shade. These plants tolerate dry soil once established.

Tips

Elderberries can be used in a shrub or mixed border, in a natural woodland garden or next to a pond or other water feature. Plants with interesting or colorful foliage can be used as specimen plants or focal points.

Recommended

S. canadensis (American elderberry), *S. nigra* (European elderberry, black elderberry), *S. racemosa* (European red elderberry) are rounded shrubs with white or pinkish white flowers followed by red or dark purple berries. Cultivars are available with green, yellow, bronze or purple foliage, and deeply divided feathery foliage. *S. canadensis* and *S. nigra* are hardy to zone 4.

Although elderberries do not require pruning, they can become scraggly and untidy if ignored.

Also called: elder **Features:** large, bushy, deciduous shrub; white or pinkish white early-summer flowers; fruit; foliage **Height:** 5–20' **Spread:** 5–20' **Hardiness:** zones 3–9

Elm

Ulmus

Dutch elm disease wiped out millions of elms across North America, but it didn't take them all. From the trees that shrugged off the attack, new, disease-resistant elms have been developed, meaning that today you can plant elms with confidence.

Growing

Elms grow well in **full sun** or **partial shade**. They adapt to most soil types and conditions but prefer a **moist, fertile** soil. They are tolerant of urban conditions, including salt from roadways.

Tips

Elms are often large trees, and are attractive where they have plenty of room to grow on large properties and in parks. Smaller species and cultivars make attractive specimen and shade trees.

Recommended

U. americana (American elm) is a large, long-lived, vase-shaped native tree with pendulous branches and shiny, dark green foliage that turns golden yellow in fall. 'New Harmony,' 'Princeton' and 'Valley Forge' are disease-resistant cultivars.

Breeding and propagation have produced a number of wonderful hybrids that offer good to excellent disease and pest resistance. 'Homestead' is hardy to zone 5. 'Morton' (ACCOLADE), 'Morton Glossy' (TRIUMPH), 'Morton Red Tip' (DANADA CHARM), 'Morton Stalwart' (COMMENDATION) and University of Wisconsin introductions 'Cathedral' and 'Regal' are hardy to zone 4.

U. 'Morton' ACCOLADE (above), U. americana (below)

A single elm tree on the south side of the house can provide the same summer cooling as many models of air-conditioning units.

Features: variable, rounded to vase-shaped, deciduous tree; fall color; bark **Height:** 40–80' **Spread:** 30–60' **Hardiness:** zones 2–9

Euonymus
Euonymus

E. alatus 'Cole's Select' (above), *E. fortunei* 'Emerald 'n' Gold' (below)

Of the trees and shrubs that can be grown by northern gardeners, only a handful match the breathtaking fall color of *E. alatus*. It's arresting in summer as well, with arching, textured branches that host delicate, soft green foliage.

Growing
Euonymus species prefer **full sun** but tolerate light or partial shade. Soil of **average to rich fertility** is preferable, but any **moist, well-drained** soil will do.

Tips
E. alatus can be grown in a shrub or mixed border, as a specimen, in a naturalistic garden or as a hedge. Dwarf cultivars can be used to create informal hedges. *E. fortunei* can be grown as a shrub in borders or as a hedge. It is an excellent substitute for the more demanding boxwood. The trailing habit also makes it useful as a groundcover or climber.

Recommended
E. alatus (burning bush, winged euonymus) is an attractive, open, mounding, deciduous shrub with vivid red fall foliage. Winter interest is provided by the corky ridges, or wings, that grow on the stems and branches. Cultivars are available.

E. fortunei (wintercreeper euonymus) is rarely grown in favor of the wide and attractive variety of cultivars. These can be prostrate, climbing or mounding evergreens, often with attractive, variegated foliage.

Features: deciduous and evergreen shrub, small tree, groundcover or climber; foliage; corky stems (E. alatus) **Height:** 2–20' **Spread:** 2–20' **Hardiness:** zones 4–8

False Cypress
Chamaecyparis

C. pisifera 'Mops' (above), C. nootkatensis 'Pendula' (below)

*C*hamaecyparis is a splendid genus of eye-catching trees and shrubs that are starting to catch on with homeowners across Minnesota and Wisconsin.

Growing

False cypresses prefer **full sun**. The soil should be **fertile, moist, neutral to acidic** and **well drained**. Alkaline soils are tolerated. In shaded areas, growth may be sparse or thin. Avoid severe pruning because new growth will not sprout from old wood. To tidy the shrubs, pull dry, brown leaves from the base by hand.

Tips

Tree varieties are used as specimen plants and for hedging. The dwarf and slow-growing cultivars are used in borders and rock gardens and as bonsai. False cypress shrubs can be grown near the house or as evergreen specimens in large containers.

Recommended

There are several available species of false cypress and many cultivars. The scaly foliage can be in a drooping or strand form, in fan-like or feathery sprays and may be dark green, bright green or gold-yellow. Plant forms vary from mounding or rounded to tall and pyramidal or narrow with pendulous branches. Check with your local garden center or nursery to see what is available.

The oils in the foliage of false cypresses may be irritating to sensitive skin.

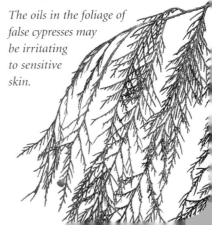

Features: narrow, pyramidal, evergreen tree or shrub; foliage; cones **Height:** 10"–100' **Spread:** 1–55' **Hardiness:** zones 3–8

Fir

Abies

A. concolor 'Candicans' (above), *A. balsamea* (below)

Welcome to the wonderful world of *Abies*, in which you will find many varieties of attractive and unusual evergreen trees sure to add arresting splendor to any northern landscape.

Growing

Firs prefer **full sun** but tolerate partial shade. The soil should be **rich, neutral to acidic, cool, moist** and **well drained**. *A. balsamea* tolerates wet soil. *A. concolor* prefers loose, sandy soil and does not tolerate heavy clay. Firs generally don't tolerate extreme heat or polluted, urban conditions, but *A. concolor* is more tolerant than other *Abies* species.

Tips

Firs make impressive specimen trees in large areas. Dwarf cultivars provide year-round interest and add distinction to mixed shrub borders, foundation plantings and perennial gardens.

Recommended

A. balsamea (balsam fir) looks pyramidal when it's young but narrows as it ages. (Zones 3–6)

A. concolor (white fir) is a large, pyramidal to conic tree. The needles have a whitish coating, giving the tree a hazy blue appearance. Cultivars with even whiter needles are available.

A. koreana (Korean fir) is a slow-growing, smaller evergreen tree bearing unusual, attractive purple-blue cones. Cultivars with attractive foliage and different forms are available. (Zones 4–7)

A. lasiocarpa (alpine fir, subalpine fir) is a slow-growing columnar to narrowly cone-shaped tree. (Zones 4–6)

Features: narrow, pyramidal or columnar, evergreen tree or shrub; foliage; cones
Height: 1–80' **Spread:** 2–30'
Hardiness: zones 3–7

Fringe Tree
Chionanthus

C. virginicus (above & below)

Although it may take a bit of extra effort to locate a nursery that stocks fringe trees, you will not regret purchasing and planting them.

Growing
Fringe trees prefer **full sun** but will grow in partial shade. They do best in soil that is **fertile, moist** and **well drained** but adapt to most soil conditions. Fringe trees appreciate regular watering and benefit greatly from winter mulching. In the wild they are often found growing alongside stream banks.

Tips
Fringe trees work well as specimen plants, as part of a border or beside a water feature. Plants begin flowering at a very early age. Both male and female plants must be present for the females to set fruit. Some trees have both male and female flowers.

Recommended
C. retusus (Chinese fringe tree) is a rounded, spreading shrub or small tree with deeply furrowed, peeling bark and erect, fragrant, white flower clusters. It is hardy only to zone 5.

C. virginicus (white fringe tree) is a spreading, small tree or large shrub that bears drooping, fragrant, white flowers.

Features: rounded or spreading, deciduous, large shrub or small tree; white early-summer flowers; fall and winter fruit; bark
Height: 10–25' **Spread:** 10–25'
Hardiness: zones 4–9

Hawthorn
Crataegus

C. laevigata (above), *C. laevigata* 'Paul's Scarlet' (below)

Interested in unusual choices for small, flowering trees for prime placement? Take a long look at the hawthorns. They are spectacular ornamental trees for hot, sunny spots.

Growing
Hawthorns grow well in **full sun**. They adapt to any **well-drained** soil, are moderate to low water users and tolerate urban conditions.

Tips
Hawthorns can be grown as specimen plants or hedges in urban sites, lakeside gardens and exposed locations. As a hedge, hawthorns create an almost impenetrable barrier.

These trees are small enough to include in most gardens. But with their long, sharp thorns, hawthorns might not be a good selection if there are children about.

Recommended
Many good species and cultivars of hawthorns are available. *C. crus-galli* 'Inermis' (var. *inermis*) is a thornless selection featuring horizontal branching and good disease resistance. *C.* × *mordenensis* is a dense, upright tree whose cultivars are hardy, attractive, and highly resistant to cedar-apple rust. *C. viridis* 'Winter King' has an attractive rounded to vase-shaped habit and dense growth. Other good hawthorns include *C. ambigua* (Russian hawthorn), *C. laevigata* (*C. oxycantha*; English hawthorn), *C.* × *nitida* (glossy hawthorn), which is often thornless, and *C. punctata* (dotted hawthorn).

Features: rounded, deciduous trees, often with a zigzagged, layered branch pattern; white to dark pink late-spring or early-summer flowers; fruit; foliage; thorny branches **Height:** 15–40' **Spread:** 12–40' **Hardiness:** zones 3–7

Honeysuckle

Lonicera

Honeysuckles are long-lived, drought resistant and easy to grow, so it's no wonder they have graced northern gardens for many generations.

Growing

Honeysuckles grow well in **full sun** and tolerate partial shade. The soil should be **average to fertile** and **well drained**.

Honeysuckles benefit from annual thinning (renewal pruning) after flowering is complete. Trim hedges twice a year (usually in early summer and again in mid- to late summer) to keep them neat.

Tips

Honeysuckles can be used in mixed borders and naturalized gardens. They make marvelous clipped or informal deciduous hedges and windbreaks. Most are large and take up a lot of space when mature.

Recommended

L. fragrantissima (winter honey-suckle, sweet breath of spring) is a large, bushy, deciduous or semi-evergreen shrub.

L. HONEY BABY ('Novso') is a stout, smaller, bushy shrub with shiny green foliage. (Zones 4–8)

L. × 'Honey Rose' is a large shrub with dark blue-green foliage.

L. tatarica (above & below)

L. tatarica (Tatarian honeysuckle) is a large, bushy, suckering shrub that is hardy to zone 3.

L. × *xylosteoides* is an erect, well-branched shrub.

L. xylosteum (European fly honeysuckle) has arching branches and gray-green foliage. It is well adapted to growing in urban conditions.

Honeysuckle flowers are often pleasantly scented, and they attract hummingbirds as well as bees and other pollinating insects.

Features: deciduous or semi-evergreen; rounded, upright shrub; creamy white, white, red, pink spring to summer, often-fragrant, flowers; fruit **Height:** 3–12' **Spread:** 3–12' **Hardiness:** zones 4–9

Horsechestnut

Aesculus

A. glabra (above), A. × carnea (below)

Growing

Horsechestnuts grow well in **full sun** or **partial shade**. The soil should be **fertile, moist** and **well drained**. These trees dislike drought.

Tips

Large horsechestnuts are used as specimen and shade trees. They create heavy shade—excellent for cooling buildings but difficult to grow grass beneath. The roots can break up sidewalks and patios if planted too close.

The smaller, shrubby horse-chestnuts can be used as specimens, in shrub or mixed borders, in mass plantings to fill unused corners or to cover hard-to-mow banks.

*A*esculus is a diverse genus of extremely attractive trees and shrubs featuring attractive foliage, billowing forms and a wide selection of sizes, habits and bloom colors.

All parts of Aesculus *plants, especially the seeds, are toxic.*

Recommended

A. × *arnoldiana* 'Autumn Splendor' is a medium tree. (Zones 4–8)

A. × *carnea* (red horsechestnut) is a dense, rounded to spreading tree. (Zones 4–8)

A. flava (*A. octandra*; yellow buckeye) is a large tree. (Zones 3–8)

A. glabra (Ohio buckeye) is a rounded tree with a dense canopy. (Zones 3–7)

A. hippocastanum (common horsechestnut) is a large, rounded tree. (Zones 3–7)

A. parviflora (bottlebrush buckeye) is a spreading, mound-forming, suckering shrub. (Zones 4–9)

A. pavia (red buckeye) is a low-growing to rounded shrubby tree that needs consistent moisture. (Zones 4–8)

Features: rounded or spreading, deciduous tree or shrub; white, yellow, red early-summer flowers; foliage; spiny fruit
Height: 8–75' **Spread:** 8–50' **Hardiness:** zones 3–9

Hydrangea

Hydrangea

H. arborescens 'Annabelle' (above), *H. paniculata* 'Grandiflora' (below)

Hydrangeas offer a bountiful mix of worthy, blooming shrubs to the northern plant palette.

Growing

Hydrangeas grow well in **full sun** or **partial shade**. *H. arborescens* tolerates heavy shade. Shade or partial shade will reduce leaf and flower scorch in the hotter regions. The soil should be of **average to high fertility, humus rich, moist** and **well drained**. These plants perform best in cool, moist conditions.

Tips

Hydrangeas can be included in shrub or mixed borders, used as specimens or informal barriers and planted in groups or containers.

Features: deciduous, mounding or spreading shrub or tree; showy, white, pink, blue flowers; foliage **Height:** 3–25' **Spread:** 3–20' **Hardiness:** zones 3–8

Recommended

H. arborescens (smooth hydrangea) is a rounded shrub that flowers well, even in shade. Its cultivars bear large clusters of showy, white blossoms.

H. macrophylla (bigleaf hydrangea) is a rounded or mounding shrub that bears pink or blue flowers and is hardy to zone 5. Many cultivars are available. ENDLESS SUMMER is reliably hardy to zone 4.

H. paniculata (panicle hydrangea) is a spreading to upright large shrub or small tree that bears white flowers. 'Grandiflora' (Peegee hydrangea) is a popular cultivar.

H. macrophylla blooms on old wood (last year's bud set), which is why blooming is spotty or nonexistent following severe winters. *H. arborescens and H. paniculata bloom on new wood, which is why they bloom every year.*

Juniper
Juniperus

J. virginiana 'Blue Arrow' (above), *J. horizontalis* 'Blue Prince' (below)

The cream indeed rises to the top, as evidenced by the long-standing and wide use of junipers in all manners of landscapes across the North. Junipers are extremely durable, evergreen shrubs.

The sometimes prickly foliage gives some gardeners a rash.

Growing

Junipers prefer **full sun** but tolerate light shade. The soil should be of **average fertility** and **well drained**, but these plants tolerate most conditions.

Tips

Junipers make excellent barriers, hedges and windbreaks. They can be used in borders, as specimens or in groups. The low-growing species can be used in rock gardens and as groundcover.

Recommended

Junipers vary from species to species and often from cultivar to cultivar within a species. *J. chinensis* (Chinese juniper) is a conical tree or spreading shrub. *J. communis* (common juniper) is a spreading shrub or a small, columnar tree. *J. horizontalis* (creeping juniper) is a prostrate, creeping ground-cover. *J. procumbens* (Japanese garden juniper) is a wide-spreading, low shrub. *J. sabina* (savin juniper) is a spreading to erect shrub. *J. scopulorum* (Rocky Mountain juniper) can be upright, rounded, weeping or spreading. *J. squamata* (singleseed juniper) forms a prostrate or low, spreading shrub or a small, upright tree. *J. virginiana* (eastern redcedar) is durable tree, upright or wide-spreading.

Features: conical or columnar tree, rounded or spreading shrub, prostrate groundcover; evergreen; foliage; variety of color, size and habit **Height:** 4"–70' **Spread:** 1–25' **Hardiness:** zones 2–9

Kentucky Coffee Tree

Gymnocladus

This splendid native is finally receiving the attention it deserves, and it should be given serious consideration when choosing a large shade tree. It matures into an elegant, billowy, feathered cloud of beauty that will be much admired for years to come.

Growing

Kentucky coffee tree grows best in **full sun**. It prefers **fertile, moist, well-drained** soil but adapts to a range of conditions, tolerating alkaline soil, drought and urban situations. Take note, Kentucky coffee tree might not leaf out until mid-May.

Tips

Ideal for spacious landscapes, parks and golf courses, Kentucky coffee tree makes an attractive specimen tree. Kentucky coffee tree has somewhat brittle branches that may be subject to wind damage.

Recommended

G. dioicus has striking bluish green foliage with rich yellow fall color and bears large clusters of white flowers. The ridged bark adds interest to the winter landscape. '**Espresso**' is an upright, vase-like, male tree with arching branches. '**J.C. McDaniel**' (PRAIRIE TITAN) is a male clone with an upright, spreading habit and a wonderful winter form. '**Stately Manor**' is another upright, vase-like, male tree that was introduced by the Minnesota Landscape Arboretum.

G. dioicus (above & below)

Kentucky coffee tree rarely suffers from pest or disease problems.

Features: upright to spreading, deciduous tree; summer and fall foliage; fruit; bark
Height: 50–75' **Spread:** 20–50'
Hardiness: zones 3–8

Lilac
Syringa

S. *meyeri* (above), S. *vulgaris* (below)

We love our lilacs in the North. Take your time while choosing one, and take care to plant lilacs where existing trees won't shade them in the decades to come.

Growing
Lilacs grow best in **full sun**. The soil should be **fertile, humus rich** and **well drained**. These plants tolerate open, windy locations.

Tips
Include lilacs in a shrub or mixed border or use them to create an informal hedge. Japanese tree lilac can be used as a specimen tree.

Recommended
The following is a severely shortened list of very good lilac species. There are literally hundreds of cultivars. Check with your garden center to see what is available.

S. × *hyacinthiflora* (hyacinth-flowered lilac, early-flowering lilac) are hardy, upright hybrids that spread as they mature.

S. meyeri (Meyer lilac) is a compact, rounded shrub.

S. patula (Manchurian lilac) is a hardy lilac with very few suckers. **'Miss Kim'** is denser in habit.

S. × *prestoniae* (Preston hybrid lilacs) is a group of very hardy, non-suckering, upright hybrids.

S. reticulata (Japanese tree lilac) is a large, rounded shrub or small tree that bears white flowers.

S. vulgaris (French lilac, common lilac) is a suckering, spreading shrub with an irregular habit.

Features: rounded or suckering, deciduous shrub or small tree; white, pink, red, magenta, purple late-spring to mid-summer flowers; easy to grow **Height:** 3–30' **Spread:** 3–30' **Hardiness:** zones 2–8

Linden

Tilia

Lindens are well-proportioned, trouble-free trees and are among the fastest growing of all large deciduous trees.

Growing

Lindens grow best in **full sun**. The soil should be **average to fertile, moist** and **well drained**. These trees adapt to most pH levels but prefer an **alkaline** soil. *T. cordata* tolerates pollution and urban conditions better than the other lindens listed here.

Tips

Lindens are useful and attractive street trees, shade trees and specimen trees. Their tolerance of pollution and their moderate size make lindens ideal for city gardens.

Recommended

There are good cultivars of most species available.

T. americana (basswood, American linden) is hardy to zone 2; its cultivars are less hardy.

T. cordata (littleleaf linden) is a dense, pyramidal tree that may become rounded with age.

T. mongolica (Mongolian linden) is a small, elegant tree with a rounded crown.

T. platyphyllos (bigleaf linden) is a large, broadly pyramidal to columnar tree that tolerates wind, salt and air pollution.

T. tomentosa (silver linden) has a broad pyramidal or rounded habit that has glossy, green leaves with fuzzy, silvery undersides. It is hardy to zone 4.

T. cordata (above), T. platyphyllos (below)

The flowers exude a dripping honeydew that will coat anything underneath, so don't plant lindens near a driveway.

Features: dense, pyramidal to rounded, deciduous tree; fragrant yellow flowers; foliage **Height:** 25–80' **Spread:** 20–60' **Hardiness:** zones 3–8

Magnolia
Magnolia

M. stellata (above), *M. de Vos-Kosar hybrid 'Betty'* (below)

Today, planting magnolias in the zone 3b–4 landscape is not only possible, it is highly recommended. These stunning shrubs and small trees lend an air of dignified elegance to the yard or garden.

Growing

Magnolias grow well in **full sun** or **partial shade.** The soil should be **fertile, humus rich, acidic, moist** and **well drained.** A 5–6" layer of mulch will help keep the roots cool and the soil moist.

Tips

Magnolias are used as specimen trees and the smaller species can be used in borders.

The flowers and young foliage may be damaged by a late frost. Avoid planting magnolias where the spring sun can encourage the blooms to open too early in the season. Cold, wind and rain can damage the blossoms.

Recommended

Many species, hybrids and cultivars in a range of sizes and with differing flowering times and flower colors are available; check with your local nursery or garden center. **M. de Vos–Kosar Hybrids** (Little Girl Hybrids, The Girl Magnolias) flower later than many other magnolias and are less likely to suffer frost damage. **M. × *loebneri* 'Merrill'** is hardy to zone 3. **M. *stellata*** (star magnolia) is a compact, bushy or spreading, deciduous shrub or small tree with many-petaled, fragrant, white flowers.

Consistent blooming is best achieved by planting magnolias in sunny, sheltered locations.

Features: upright to spreading, deciduous shrub or tree; showy, fragrant, pink, white, yellow flowers; fruit; foliage; bark **Height:** 8–40' **Spread:** 8–30' **Hardiness:** zones 3–8

Maple

Acer

The maples form a very large group of diverse and varied trees that offer wonderful foliage, stellar form and fiery fall color.

Growing

Generally maples do well in **full sun** or **light shade,** though this varies from species to species. The soil should be **fertile, moist, high in organic matter** and **well drained**.

Tips

Maples can be used as specimen trees, as large elements in shrub or mixed borders or as hedges. Some are useful as understory plants bordering wooded areas; others can be grown in containers on patios or terraces. Few Japanese gardens are without the attractive smaller maples. Maples are popular shade or street trees. Almost all maples can be used to create bonsai specimens.

A. ginnala 'Bailey Compact' (above), *A. griseum* (below)

Recommended

Many maples are very large when fully mature, but there are also a few smaller species that are useful in smaller gardens, including *A. campestre* (hedge maple), *A. ginnala* (amur maple), *A. griseum* (paperbark maple), *A. pensylvanicum* (striped maple, moosewood), *A. pseudosieboldianum* (Korean maple, purplebloom maple) and *A. tataricum* (Tatarian maple). Check with your local nursery or garden center for availability.

Maple fruits, called samaras, have wings that act like miniature helicopter rotors and help in seed dispersal.

Features: small, multi-stemmed, deciduous tree or large shrub; foliage; bark; winged fruit; fall color; form; flowers **Height:** 5–80' **Spread:** 5–70' **Hardiness:** zones 2–9, varies with the species

Mountain Ash

Sorbus

S. aucuparia (above), S. americana (below)

Mountain ashes quickly develop extremely handsome, rounded-to-oval forms and varied bark coloration. However, the prime values of these trees are their wonderful flowers and fruits.

Mountain ashes are susceptible to fire blight and borers.

Growing

Grow mountain ashes in **full sun, partial shade** or **light shade** in **humus-rich, average to fertile, moist, well-drained** soil.

Tips

Use mountain ashes as specimens in small gardens, or plant them in woodland and natural gardens. They can attract a variety of wildlife.

Recommended

S. alnifolia (Korean mountain ash) is a broad, pyramidal to rounded tree. It has golden yellow fall color and persistent red to pink-red fruit. (Zones 4–8)

S. americana (American mountain ash) is an oval to rounded tree or large shrub that has yellow to red fall color and orange to red fruit.

S. aucuparia (European mountain ash) is a pollution-tolerant, single- to multi-stemmed, floriferous tree with a low, rounded crown and red to orange fall color. Good cultivars are available. (Zones 3–7)

S. decora (showy mountain ash) is an upright tree or large shrub with dark blue-green foliage that turns orange-red in fall. The spherical fruit is bright red.

S. hybrida is a vigorous, erect tree, which, when mature, becomes broadly pyramidal with wide, spreading branches and deeply lobed, dark blue-green, oak-like foliage. (Zones 4–8)

Features: rounded to broadly pyramidal, single- or multi-stemmed, deciduous tree; form; white flowers; foliage; fruit **Height:** 15–40' **Spread:** 10–30' **Hardiness:** zones 2–8

Ninebark
Physocarpus

P. opulifolius 'Dart's Gold' (above), *P. opulifolius* DIABOLO 'Monlo' (below)

Ninebark is a tough-as-nails plant that features attractive foliage and eye-popping, early-summer flowers.

Growing

Ninebark grows well in **full sun** or **partial shade**. The best leaf coloring develops in a sunny location. The soil should be **fertile, moist** and **well drained**. It adapts well to alkaline soil.

Tips

Ninebark is an easy-to-grow shrub that adapts to most garden conditions. It can be included in a shrub or mixed border, in a woodland garden or in a naturalistic garden.

Recommended

P. opulifolius (common ninebark) is a suckering shrub with long, arching branches and exfoliating bark. It bears light pink flowers in early summer, and fruit that ripens to reddish green in fall. Several cultivars are available. **'Dart's Gold'** and **'Nugget'** bear bright yellow foliage. DIABOLO ('Monlo') has attractive purple foliage. SUMMER WINE ('Seward') has dark crimson foliage. **'Nanus'** (var. *nanus*; dwarf ninebark) is a bushy, dwarf shrub with small, dark green leaves. **'Snowfall'** has more, and larger, clusters of flowers than the species.

You may not actually find nine layers, but the peeling, flecked bark of ninebark does add interest to the winter landscape.

Features: upright, sometimes suckering, deciduous shrub; light pink early to mid-summer flowers; fruit; bark; foliage **Height:** 2–10' **Spread:** 2–15' **Hardiness:** zones 2–8

Oak

Quercus

Q. macrocarpa (above)

Oaks define the concept of majesty. Their form, foliage, bark and fall color are hard to beat when a large shade tree is desired.

Growing

Oaks grow well in **full sun** or **partial shade**. The soil should be **fertile, moist** and **well drained**. Most oaks prefer slightly acidic soils but adapt to alkaline conditions (except for *Q. palustris*). Oaks can be difficult to establish; transplant them only while they are young.

Tips

Oaks are large trees that are best as specimens or for groves in parks and large gardens. Do not disturb the ground around the base of an oak; it is very sensitive to changes in grade.

Recommended

There are many oaks to choose from. A few popular species are *Q. alba* (white oak), a rounded, spreading tree with peeling bark and purple-red fall color; *Q. bicolor* (swamp white oak), a broad, spreading tree that has peeling bark and orange or red fall color; *Q.* × *bimundorum* CRIMSON SPIRE ('Crimschmidt'), the best oak for small lots; and *Q. macrocarpa* (bur oak, mossycup oak), which is the hardiest of the oaks, to zone 2. Some cultivars are available. Check with your local nursery or garden center.

Features: large, rounded, spreading, deciduous tree; summer and fall foliage; bark; acorns **Height:** 40–100' **Spread:** 15–100' **Hardiness:** zones 3–9

Pine
Pinus

Pines are essential to northern landscapes, not just for their unmatched winter beauty but also for their ability to serve as majestic, evergreen anchors.

Growing
Pines grow best in **full sun**. They are not heavy feeders, but soil of **moderate fertility** is recommended. They adapt to most **well-drained** soils. *P. flexilis* tolerates partial shade and needs moist, well-drained soil.

Tips
Pines are more diverse and widely adapted than other conifers. Pines can be used as specimen trees, as hedges or to create windbreaks. Smaller cultivars can be included in shrub or mixed borders. These trees are not heavy feeders; fertilizing will encourage rapid new growth that is weak and susceptible to pest and disease problems.

Recommended
There are many available pines, both trees and shrubby dwarf plants. Check with your local garden center or nursery to find out what is in stock.

The Austrian pine, *P. nigra*, was often recommended as the most urban-tolerant pine, but overplanting has led to severe disease problems, some of which can kill a tree in a single growing season.

P. ponderosa (above), P. strobus (below)

Pines offer exciting possibilities for any garden. Exotic-looking pines are available with soft or stiff needles, needles with yellow bands, trunks with patterned or mother-of-pearl-like bark and varied forms.

Features: upright, columnar or spreading, evergreen tree; foliage; bark; cones **Height:** 1–120' **Spread:** 2–50' **Hardiness:** zones 2–8

Poplar & Aspen
Populus

P. tremula 'Erecta' (above & below)

Although some noted experts suggest that *Populus* species be left in the wild, their extremely fast growth rate makes them worthy of some consideration.

Plant them well back from water pipes, drains and building foundations, which can be damaged by the roots.

Growing

Poplars and aspens grow best in **full sun** in **deep, fertile, moist, well-drained** soil. They adapt to a wide range of soils and are pollution tolerant.

Tips

Poplars and aspens are large, fast-growing trees useful for naturalizing, in shelterbelts, and on large, open properties. Narrow selections are used as screens and in tight spots.

These trees tend to drop their twigs and foliage, and the female plants often shed copious amounts of fluffy seed.

Recommended

There are several available species of poplar and aspen. Check with your local garden center or nursery to see what is available.

P. deltoides 'Siouxland' (cottonless cottonwood) is a large tree with a broad, open, irregular crown and massive, spreading branches. It is a seedless, rust-resistant selection.

P. × 'Griffin' is a narrow, pyramidal, seedless clone with ascending branches and dark green foliage.

P. nigra 'Italica' (var. *italica*; Lombardy poplar) is a short-lived, narrow, columnar, seedless tree with sharply ascending branches.

P. tremula 'Erecta' (Swedish columnar aspen, European columnar aspen) is a narrow, densely branched, spire-like, seedless tree.

Also called: cottonwood **Features:** fast, dense growth; rounded, upright or narrow, deciduous trees **Height:** 30–120' **Spread:** 6–75' **Hardiness:** zones 1–9

Redbud
Cercis

Of you're looking for a small tree that provides glorious spring blooms, a wonderful layered form and bold, unusual foliage, plant a redbud.

Growing

Redbud grows well in full sun (if given excellent soil preparation and regular watering) but is best in **partial shade** or **light shade**. The soil should be a **fertile, deep loam** that is **moist** and **well drained**. Mix up to **20% organic matter**, such as compost, into the soil in and around the planting area. Water whenever the top 2" of soil has dried. Mulch with a 3–4" layer of pine needles or wood chips. Plant in spring only. Redbud has tender roots and dislikes being transplanted.

Tips

Redbud can be used as a specimen tree, in a shrub or mixed border or in a woodland garden. Its greatest function is as a focal point in partial, or even full (not dense), shade.

Recommended

C. canadensis (eastern redbud) is a spreading, multi-stemmed tree that bears red, purple or pink flowers. The young foliage is bronze, fading to green over the summer and turning bright yellow in fall. Look for the **Minnesota Strain** or **Wisconsin Strain** varieties.

C. canadensis (above & below)

Redbud can be long-lived if the tree's suckers are allowed to develop and replace the original trunk.

Features: rounded or spreading, multi-stemmed, deciduous tree or shrub; red, purple, pink spring flowers; fall foliage; good form **Height:** 20–30' **Spread:** 25–35' **Hardiness:** zones 4–9

Rhododendron • Azalea
Rhododendron

R. 'Purple Gem' (above), azalea hybrid (below)

Among the most beautiful of all flowering shrubs, *Rhododendron* species grace the landscape with large, sensual blooms in spring and attractive form and foliage throughout the growing season.

Growing

Rhododendrons prefer **partial shade** or **light shade**. Deciduous azaleas perform best in **full sun** or **light shade**. Evergreen azaleas appreciate **partial shade**. Provide **shelter** from strong winds. The soil should be **fertile, humus rich, acidic** (pH of 4.5–6.0), **moist** and very **well drained**. These plants are very sensitive to salt and drought.

In heavy soils, elevate the crown 1" above the soil level when planting to ensure surface drainage of excess water. Don't dig near rhododendrons and azaleas; they resent root disturbance.

Tips

Use rhododendrons and azaleas in shrub or mixed borders, in woodland gardens, as specimen plants, in group plantings, as hedges and informal barriers, in rock gardens or in planters on a shady patio or balcony.

Recommended

In Minnesota and Wisconsin, we can grow many different rhododendron and azalea species and cultivars. Nurseries and specialty growers can help you find the right plant to suit your taste and garden.

Features: upright, mounding, rounded, evergreen or deciduous shrub; white, pink, purple, cream, salmon, red, bicolored late-winter to early-summer flowers; foliage **Height:** 1–10' **Spread:** 2–10' **Hardiness:** zones 3–9

Russian Cypress
Microbiota

M. decussata (above & below)

Oh, now we're talking! Russian cypress is an exquisite, extremely cold-hardy, low-growing evergreen shrub that is finally getting the attention it deserves.

Growing

Russian cypress grows best in **partial to nearly full shade** in **moderately fertile, well-drained** soil. In poorly drained soil it can die from root rot. It prefers cool conditions but struggles in dense shade. It does well in full sun, with mulching and regular watering. Russian cypress tolerates windy sites and adapts to poor, dry soil if the drainage is good.

Don't freak out in fall when the entire plant turns plum-colored. That's just a nice late-season bonus.

Also called: Russian arborvitae, Siberian cypress **Features:** wide-spreading, prostrate, evergreen shrub; summer and winter foliage; form **Height:** 12–18" **Spread:** 6–10' **Hardiness:** zones 2–8

Tips

Russian cypress makes an excellent ground-cover and can be used for erosion control on slopes. It cascades gracefully down walls and raised planters and is also a good substitute for prostrate junipers and yews. It can be used in shrub beds and rock gardens but may be too large for that purpose.

Recommended

M. decussata is a slow-growing evergreen shrub that has wide-spreading, prostrate branches with pendent branch tips. Flattened splays of bright green foliage gradually darken over summer and become an attractive reddish brown to bronze-purple in winter. In spring the green color quickly returns.

Serviceberry

Amelanchier

A. canadensis (above), A. laevis (below)

These tough, easy-to-grow shrubs include a number of native varieties that are splendid in informal mass plantings and can be stunning in formal settings.

Growing

Serviceberries grow well in **full sun** or **light shade**. They prefer **acidic** soil that is **fertile, humus rich, moist** and **well drained**, but they do adjust to drought.

Tips

Use serviceberries as specimens or shade trees in small gardens. Grow shrubby forms along woodland edges or in borders. Serviceberries are beautiful beside ponds or streams.

Recommended

Several species and hybrids are available. *A. alnifolia* (serviceberry, Saskatoon, Juneberry) is a native shrub. *A. arborea* (downy serviceberry, Juneberry) is a small, single- or multi-stemmed tree. *A. canadensis* (shadblow serviceberry) is a large, upright, suckering shrub with good fall color. *A. × grandiflora* (apple serviceberry) is a small, spreading, often multi-stemmed tree. *A. laevis* (Allegheny serviceberry) is a tree with a spreading habit. *A. × lamarckii* (Lamarck's service-berry) is an erect, multi-stemmed shrub or small tree.

Serviceberry fruit can be used in place of blueberries in any recipe. The fruit has a similar but generally sweeter flavor.

Also called: saskatoon, Juneberry
Features: single- or multi-stemmed, deciduous, large shrub or small tree; white spring or early-summer flowers; edible, purple to blue-black fruit; fall color; bark **Height:** 3–30'
Spread: 3–30' **Hardiness:** zones 2–9

Spirea
Spiraea

S. japonica 'Goldmound' (above), *S.* × *vanhouttei* (below)

If you are looking for durable, easy-to-grow, profusely blooming small shrubs to use in formal or semi-formal foundation plantings, look no further than *Spiraea*.

Growing

Spireas prefer **full sun**. To help prevent foliage burn, provide protection from very hot sun. The soil should be **fertile, acidic, moist** and **well drained**.

Pruning is necessary if you prefer plants to be tidy. The tight, shrubby types require less pruning than the larger, more open forms. Pruning information for spirea and the other trees, shrubs and woody plants mentioned in this book can be found in the Lone Pine gardening guide, *Tree & Shrub Gardening for Minnesota and Wisconsin*.

Features: round, bushy, deciduous shrub; pink or white summer flowers
Height: 6"–10' **Spread:** 1–12'
Hardiness: zones 3–9

Tips

Spireas are used in shrub or mixed borders, in rock gardens and as informal screens and hedges.

Recommended

Many species and cultivars of spirea are available, including the following two very popular selections. *S. japonica* (Japanese spirea) forms a clump of erect stems and bears pink or white flowers. It is parent to a plethora of colorful cultivars. *S.* × *vanhouttei* (bridal wreath spirea, Vanhoutte spirea) is a dense, bushy shrub with arching branches that bears clusters of white flowers. Check at your local nursery or garden center to see what is available.

Under a magnifying glass, the flowers of these rose family members do indeed resemble tiny roses.

Spruce
Picea

P. glauca 'Conica' (above), P. pungens var. glauca 'Moerheim' (below)

Growing

Spruce grow best in **full sun** in **neutral to acidic, deep, well-drained** soil. Spruce tolerates alkaline soil. *P. glauca* 'Conica' prefers light shade and a sheltered location. *P. mariana* grows in boggy and wet areas and tolerates poor soil.

These trees generally don't like hot, dry or polluted conditions. Spruces are best grown from small, young stock as they dislike being transplanted when larger or more mature.

Tips

Spruce trees are used as specimens. The dwarf and slow-growing cultivars can also be used in shrub or mixed borders. *P. mariana* is best used for reclamation and for naturalization. Spruce trees look most attractive when allowed to keep their lower branches.

Recommended

Spruce are generally upright pyramidal trees, but cultivars may be low-growing, wide-spreading or even weeping in habit. *P. abies* (Norway spruce), *P. glauca* (white spruce), *P. mariana* (black spruce, bog spruce), *P. omorika* (Serbian spruce), *P. pungens* (Colorado spruce) and their cultivars are popular and commonly available.

Oil-based pesticides such as dormant oil can take the blue out of your blue-needled spruces.

*P*icea is a large, invaluable genus that includes some of the most popular evergreen trees and shrubs for Minnesota and Wisconsin gardens.

Features: conical or columnar, evergreen tree or shrub; foliage; cones **Height:** 1–80' **Spread:** 18"–30' **Hardiness:** zones 2–8

Sumac

Rhus

R. typhina (above), R. aromatica (below)

Sumacs are long-lived, often spreading and always easy to grow. The season-long foliage displays outstanding form and color, with many varieties putting forth a stellar fall show of brilliant yellows, oranges and reds.

Growing

Sumacs develop the best fall color in **full sun** but tolerate partial shade. The soil should be of **average fertility, moist** and **well drained**. Once established, sumacs are very drought tolerant.

These plants can become invasive. Remove suckers that come up where you don't want them.

Tips

Sumacs can be used in a shrub or mixed border, in a woodland garden or on a sloping bank. Both male and female plants are needed for fruit to form.

Recommended

A number of good species and cultivars are available including *R. aromatica* (fragrant sumac; zones 3–9), *R. copallina* (shining sumac, flameleaf sumac; zones 4–9), *R. glabra* (smooth sumac; zones 2–8), *R. trilobata* (skunkbush sumac, lemonade sumac; zones 3–8) and *R. typhina* (*R. hirta*; staghorn sumac; zones 3–8). *R. typhina* '**Bailtiger**' (TIGER EYES) has finely cut, burn-resistant, golden yellow foliage.

Wear gloves when pulling up suckers to avoid getting the unusual, onion-like odor on your hands.

Features: bushy, suckering, colony-forming, deciduous shrub; summer and fall foliage; chartreuse summer flowers; fuzzy, red, fall fruit **Height:** 2–25' **Spread:** 5–25' or more; often exceeds height **Hardiness:** zones 2–9

Summersweet Clethra

Clethra

C. alnifolia 'Paniculata' (above & below)

This relatively small, charming shrub has a wide variety of uses and isn't planted nearly enough by northern gardeners. Clethra doesn't like to be dry, so give it a little extra water, and then be prepared to fall in love.

Growing

Summersweet clethra grows best in **light or partial shade**. The soil should be **fertile, humus rich, acidic, moist** and **well drained**. This plant tolerates poorly drained, organic soils. Deadhead, if possible, to keep the shrub looking neat.

Tips

This shrub tends to sucker, though not aggressively, forming a colony of stems. Use it in a border or in the light shade at the edge of a woodland garden. Try one of the new dwarf cultivars at the front of a border to better enjoy the lovely fragrance.

Summersweet clethra is useful in damp, shaded gardens, where the late-season flowers are much appreciated.

Recommended

C. alnifolia is a large, rounded, upright, colony-forming shrub that bears attractive spikes of white flowers. The foliage turns yellow in fall. Recommended cultivars include the low-growing '**Hummingbird**,' and '**Ruby Spice**,' a selection with reddish pink flowers.

Also called: sweet pepperbush, sweetspire
Features: rounded, suckering, deciduous shrub; fragrant, white summer flowers; attractive habit; colorful fall foliage
Height: 2–8' **Spread:** 3–8' **Hardiness:** zones 3–9

Viburnum
Viburnum

V. opulus (above), *V. plicatum var. tomentosum* (below)

Viburnums have been heavily used in northern landscapes for generations, and the many splendid, recently developed varieties available at nurseries today keep them as popular as ever.

Growing

Viburnums grow well in **full sun, partial shade** or **light shade**. The soil should be of **average fertility, moist** and **well drained**. Viburnums tolerate both alkaline and acidic soils.

Viburnum fruit varies in its palatability. Fruiting is generally better when more than one plant of a species is present, provided they flower at the same time, to allow for cross-pollination.

Tips

Viburnums can be used in borders and woodland gardens. They are a good choice for plantings near swimming pools.

Recommended

Over a dozen excellent viburnum species are available in Minnesota and Wisconsin, as well as a plethora of great hybrids and cultivars. Check with your local nursery or garden center to see what is available and appropriate for your garden. *V. dentatum* (arrowwood) is an upright, arching shrub that is hardy and durable. *V. trilobum* (American cranberrybush, highbush cranberry) is a dense, rounded shrub. Both species are hardy to zone 2.

Many species of birds are attracted to viburnums for the edible fruit and the shelter they provide.

Features: bushy or spreading, evergreen, semi-evergreen or deciduous shrub; white to pink flowers (some fragrant); summer and fall foliage; fruit **Height:** 2–20' **Spread:** 2–15' **Hardiness:** zones 2–9

Weigela

Weigela

W. florida WINE & ROSES ('Alexandra'; above), *W. florida* cultivar (below)

Any hot spot in full sun calls for weigela, for you will never tire of the dazzling fireworks display created by its hearty, early-summer bloom. Weigela is unsurpassed in sunny foundation plantings or when grouped to form a mid-sized, informal hedge.

Weigela is one of the longest-blooming shrubs, with the main flush of blooms lasting as long as six weeks. It often re-blooms if sheared lightly after the first flowers fade.

Growing

Weigela prefers **full sun** but tolerates partial shade. For the best leaf color, grow purple-leaved plants in full sun and yellow-leaved plants in partial shade. The soil should be **fertile** and **well drained**. Weigela adapts to most well-drained soils.

Tips

Weigelas can be used in shrub or mixed borders, in open woodland gardens and as informal barrier plantings.

Recommended

W. florida is a spreading shrub with arching branches that bears clusters of dark pink flowers. Many hybrids and cultivars are available, including dwarf varieties, red-, pink- or white-flowered varieties and varieties with purple, bronze or yellow foliage. FRENCH LACE ('Brigela') has lime green to yellow leaf margins. MIDNIGHT WINE ('Elvera') is a dwarf plant with purple foliage. WINE & ROSES ('Alexandra') has dark purple foliage.

Features: upright or low, spreading, deciduous shrub; red, pink, white late-spring to early-summer flowers; foliage **Height:** 18"–6' **Spread:** 18"–6' **Hardiness:** zones 3–8

Willow

Salix

S. integra 'Hakuro Nishiki' (above), *S. purpurea* (below)

Willows are star performers in moist areas and are ideal for naturalizing in low, marshy areas. Most varieties have curling branches that add sculptural interest in winter.

Growing

Willows generally grow best in **full sun** in **deep, moist, well-drained** soil. *S. integra* 'Hakuro Nishiki' grows well in light shade. *S. purpurea* is suitable for wet areas. The large *Salix* species and cultivars should not be planted near water supply and drainage lines, because the roots may invade the pipes and cause expensive blockages.

Tips

Willows make excellent specimen plants. The small species look great when used in shrub and mixed borders. Many willows are very effective next to water features. Use small and trailing forms in rock gardens and along retaining walls.

Recommended

There are now many popular willows available. Check with your local garden center or nursery.

S. integra '**Hakuro Nishiki**' (dappled willow, Japanese dappled willow) is a spreading shrub with arching branches and green, cream and pink variegated leaves. (Zones 5–8)

S. purpurea (purple willow, basket willow, purple osier willow) is a large, spreading shrub or small, upright tree with arching branches. (Zones 4–7)

Features: deciduous; large tree with broad, open crown, or small to large, oval to rounded shrub; summer and fall foliage; colorful young stems
Height: 6"–40' **Spread:** 3–25'
Hardiness: zones 2–8

Witch-Hazel

Hamamelis

H. virginiana (above & below)

H. virginiana is a large, native shrub found in the wild across Wisconsin and Minnesota, always an indication that the same plant purchased at the nursery likely requires little special care in your home landscape.

Growing

Witch-hazels grow best in a sheltered spot with **full sun or light shade**. The soil should be of **average fertility, neutral to acidic, moist** and **well drained**.

H. virginiana is usually the only witchhazel available at nurseries in zones 3–4. Wisconsin gardeners in zone 5 have more choices to explore, including the wonderful H. × intermedia varieties.

Tips

Witch-hazels work well as specimen plants or in groups in shrub or mixed borders, or in woodland gardens. As small trees, they are ideal for space-limited gardens.

The unique flowers have long, narrow, crinkled, spidery-looking petals when in bloom. If the weather gets too cold, the petals will roll up, protecting the flowers and extending the flowering season.

Recommended

H. × intermedia is a vase-shaped, spreading shrub. (Zones 5–9)

H. vernalis (vernal witchhazel) is a rounded, upright, often suckering shrub with very fragrant, early spring flowers. (Zones 4–8)

H. virginiana (common witchhazel) is a large, rounded, spreading shrub or small tree. (Zones 3–8)

Features: spreading, deciduous shrub or small tree; fragrant, yellow to orange early-spring flowers; summer and fall foliage
Height: 6–20' **Spread:** 6–20'
Hardiness: zones 3–9

Yew
Taxus

$\mathcal{E}$vergreens are essential for winter interest, and the recently introduced yew varieties are stellar shrubs.

Growing
Most yews grow well in any light condition from **full sun to full shade** in **fertile, moist, well-drained** soil. They generally tolerate soils of any acidity, urban pollution and windy or dry conditions. Avoid very wet soil, such as near downspouts, and areas contaminated with road salt. *T. canadensis* prefers a cool site with full shade and shelter from strong winds.

Tips
Use yews in borders or as specimens, hedges, topiary or groundcovers. Male plants must be present for most females to bear the attractive red arils (seed cups).

T. × media 'Sunburst' (above), *T. cuspidata* (below)

Recommended
T. canadensis (Canadian yew, American yew, ground-hemlock) is a mostly self-fertile, low-growing, spreading, native shrub. (Zones 2–6)

T. cuspidata (Japanese yew) is a slow-growing, broad, columnar or conical tree, primarily with dark green foliage, though the new varieties **'Dwarf Bright Gold'** and **'Nana Aurescens'** feature sunny yellow foliage.

T. × media (English Japanese yew) forms a rounded, upright tree or shrub, though the size and form varies among the many cultivars.

Features: evergreen; conical or columnar tree or bushy or spreading shrub; foliage; red seed cups **Height:** 1–50' **Spread:** 2–30' **Hardiness:** zones 4–7

Alexander Mackenzie

Explorer Shrub Rose

Alexander Mackenzie is known not only for its beauty and scent, but also for its outstanding disease resistance. It bears clusters of fragrant, brightly colored flowers throughout the summer months and well into fall.

Growing

Alexander Mackenzie prefers **full sun**. The soil should be **fertile**, **rich with organic matter**, **moist** and **well drained**.

Tips

This rose is extremely hardy, vigorous and highly resistant to powdery mildew and blackspot. It requires little maintenance. Alexander Mackenzie is suitable as a specimen plant and can be included with other roses and perennials in a mixed border.

Deadheading regularly will encourage a longer, more prolific bloom cycle.

Recommended

Rosa 'Alexander Mackenzie' is a tall, upright shrub bearing clusters of fragrant, double flowers. The thorny stems are tinged with hints of reddish purple and carry light green, serrated foliage.

Sir Alexander Mackenzie was a noted explorer and fur trader, and was the first European crossing the North American continent to discover a pass through the Rocky Mountains.

Features: hardy shrub; mild raspberry-scented, deep red with hot pink flowers in spring that repeat in fall **Height:** 5–7' **Spread:** 5–7' **Hardiness:** zones 3–8

Belle Amour

Old Garden Rose

Classified as an ancient damask rose, Belle Amour is extremely easy to grow, even in the worst soil or environmental conditions.

Growing
Belle Amour grows best in **full sun**. The soil should be **average to fertile, humus rich, slightly acidic, moist** and **well drained**, but this rose tolerates most soil conditions once established.

Tips
Old garden roses like Belle Amour seem most at home in an English country-style garden, but they can be used in borders and as specimens.

Recommended
Rosa 'Belle Amour' is an upright shrub with gray-green foliage. It bears fully double camellia-like blooms in a single flush in late spring or early summer. The bright red hips persist into winter.

Old Garden roses are those discovered or hybridized before 1867 and are admired for their delicate beauty, old-fashioned appearance and fantastic fragrance. They are the ancestors of many roses grown today.

Some claim that Belle Amour is a cross between an alba and a damask rose.

Features: upright habit; spicy myrrh-scented, light to medium pink early-summer flowers; red hips **Height:** 5–6' **Spread:** 3–4' **Hardiness:** zones 3–8

Blanc Double de Coubert

Rugosa Shrub Rose

*E*very rose garden should include one of these magnificent rugosa roses. This beautiful rose, over a century old, has a fascinating history and an outstanding reputation.

Growing
This hardy rugosa tolerates light shade but prefers **full sun.** Most soils are adequate but **organically rich, moist, well-drained** soils are best.

Tips
Blanc Double de Coubert is excellent for hedging and borders, or planted as a specimen. The blossoms are ideal for cutting as well, but cut the stems when they are still partially closed to extend the flowers' vase life.

Recommended
Rosa 'Blanc Double de Coubert' is a moderately vigorous, dense shrub with arching branches. It bears loosely petaled, semi-double, fragrant, white blossoms followed by hips that transform into reddish orange spheres and stand out among the stunning fall foliage.

The soft petals are easily marked by rain, which may cause the flowers to appear spent not long after they open.

Blanc Double de Coubert is highly resistant to disease.

Features: hardy; strongly scented, white early-summer flowers that repeat in fall **Height:** 4–7' **Spread:** 4–7' **Hardiness:** zones 3–8

Hansa

Rugosa Shrub Rose

Hansa, first introduced in 1905, is one of the most durable, long-lived and versatile roses.

Growing

Hansa grows best in **full sun**. The soil should preferably be **average to fertile, humus rich, slightly acidic, moist** and **well drained**, but this durable rose adapts to most soils, from sandy to silty clay. Remove a few of the oldest canes every few years to keep plants blooming vigorously.

Tips

Rugosa roses like Hansa make good additions to mixed borders and beds and can also be used as hedges or as specimens. They are often used on steep banks to prevent soil erosion. Their prickly branches deter people from walking across flowerbeds and compacting the soil.

Recommended

Rosa 'Hansa' is a bushy shrub with arching canes and leathery, deeply veined, bright green leaves. The double flowers are produced all summer. The bright orange hips persist into winter.

Rosa rugosa is a wide-spreading plant with disease-resistant foliage, a trait it has passed on to many hybrids and cultivars.

Features: dense, arching habit; clove-scented, mauve purple or mauve red early-summer to fall flowers; orange-red hips **Height:** 4–5'
Spread: 5–6' **Hardiness:** zones 3–8

Henry Hudson
Explorer Shrub Rose

Henry Hudson was introduced in 1976 and has proven to be easy to maintain, hardy and resistant to mildew and blackspot.

Growing
Henry Hudson grows best in **full sun** but tolerates some afternoon shade. The soil should be **average to fertile, humus rich, slightly acidic, moist** and **well drained**. Deadhead to keep plants tidy.

Tips
With its thorny, impenetrable growth, Henry Hudson makes an attractive barrier plant, hedge or groundcover. It spreads by suckers and can be used on banks to prevent soil erosion. It also looks attractive in mixed beds or borders.

Recommended
Rosa 'Henry Hudson' is a spreading, rounded shrub with bright green foliage and semi-double flowers produced profusely all summer. Roses in the Explorer Series come in a variety of flower colors and sizes, including climbers.

The Explorer roses were developed by Agriculture Canada to be cold hardy and disease resistant, making them ideal for Minnesota and Wisconsin gardens.

All the roses in this series have been named after explorers of Canada.

Features: rounded habit; clove-scented, white early-summer to fall flowers **Height:** 24–36"
Spread: 2–5' **Hardiness:** zones 2–8

Hope for Humanity
Parkland Shrub Rose

Introduced in 1995, Hope for Humanity was named in honor of the 100th anniversary of the Canadian Red Cross Society.

Growing

Hope for Humanity grows best in **full sun**. The soil should be **fertile, humus rich, slightly acidic, moist** and **well drained**.

The foliage is resistant to mildew and rust but is somewhat susceptible to blackspot.

Tips

This small, attractive plant makes a good addition to a mixed bed or border, and it is attractive when planted in groups of three or more. Its small stature also makes it a popular choice for containers and large planters, though some winter protection may be needed for plants not grown directly in the ground.

Recommended

Rosa 'Hope for Humanity' is a compact, low-growing shrub with glossy, dark green foliage and double, blood red flowers with a small, white spot at the petal base, and a white or yellow spot on the outer margin of each petal. The flowers are produced over a long period in summer. The Parkland rose series boasts a wide range of flower colors, some of which are uncommon in hardy shrub roses.

The hardy Parkland roses were developed in Brandon, Manitoba, Canada for use in prairie and northern gardens.

Features: compact habit; lightly scented, red mid-summer to fall flowers **Height:** 24" **Spread:** 24" **Hardiness:** zones 3–8

John Franklin

Explorer Shrub Rose

This rose was named after a well-known British naval officer and northern explorer remembered for his expeditions and for the highly publicized 12-year search for him and his lost ships in the mid-1800s.

John Franklin has a slightly different flowering habit than other explorer roses. It is an everblooming rose, meaning that rather than repeat blooming, it blooms continuously from summer to fall. The bright red flowers just keep coming, rain or shine, until the cool fall days finally slow it down.

Growing

John Franklin tolerates shade but prefers **partial to full sun.** The soil should be a **fertile, well-drained, moisture-holding loam** with at least 5% **organic matter.**

Tips

Its compact, bushy form makes this rose useful for hedging, borders and smaller gardens. John Franklin is ideal for those tight spaces that need a punch of color.

Recommended

Rosa 'John Franklin' bears tight buds that open to semi-double flowers. The small, fringed flowers are borne in abundant, large clusters of 30 or more. The leaves are serrated and dark green with touches of burgundy around the edges.

Features: compact, bushy form; lightly scented, medium red blossoms that bloom from spring to fall **Height:** 1–5' **Spread:** 4' **Hardiness:** zones 3–8

Macy's Pride
Modern Shrub Rose

Macy's Pride was chosen by the famous Macy's Department Store to honor the store's 100th anniversary.

Growing
Macy's Pride prefers **full sun**. The soil should be a **fertile, well-drained, moisture-holding loam** with at least 5% **organic matter**.

Tips
The uniform size and shape of Macy's Pride makes it ideal for hedges and for use in mixed borders and shrub beds. Macy's Pride also makes an excellent specimen and is at home in a formal rose garden.

Recommended
Rosa MACY'S PRIDE ('BAIcream') is a vigorous, upright shrub that bears fragrant, creamy white, double flowers that arise from lemon yellow buds. The flowers resemble those of hybrid tea roses. It blooms from June to October. The disease-resistant, semi-glossy foliage is edged in red when young.

Features: long-lasting, fragrant, creamy white flowers that bloom from spring to fall; low maintenance
Height: 4–5' **Spread:** 4–5'
Hardiness: zones 4–7

EASY ELEGANCE roses from Bailey Nurseries are beautiful, hardy, sucker-free roses that produce flowers over most of the growing season. These roses come on their own roots and have a uniform size and shape. Bailey Nurseries does not pamper these roses, ensuring that the rose you take home is tough and durable.

Martin Frobisher

Explorer Shrub Rose

In 1968, Martin Frobisher became the first rose to be introduced in the Explorer series. It has the appearance of an old rose but has a few unique physical features—the older growth is covered in reddish brown bark, the upper portions of the branches are spineless and it does not form hips.

Martin Frobisher was an Elizabethan seafaring explorer who discovered what is now known as Frobisher Bay on Baffin Island while he was searching for the Northwest Passage in 1576.

Growing

Martin Frobisher prefers at least five or six hours of **full sun** daily. The soil should be **well drained**, **slightly acidic**, **humus rich** and **moist**.

Tips

This upright shrub rose works well in mixed borders but is also effective left as a specimen.

Recommended

Rosa 'Martin Frobisher' bears intensely fragrant, double flowers that open from well-shaped buds. It is a vigorous, dense, compact, well-proportioned, pillar-shaped shrub. Dark red, smooth stems display wrinkly, grayish green leaves.

Features: tall, upright form; intensely scented, pale pink early-summer blossoms that repeat in fall **Height:** 5–6' **Spread:** 4–5' **Hardiness:** zones 2–8

Morden Fireglow

Parkland Shrub Rose

This rose is truly a favorite. One of the Parkland Series, this hardy specimen bears flowers that are neither red nor orange—a color unlike that of any hardy shrub rose.

Growing

Morden Fireglow prefers at least five to six hours of **full sun** per day. The soil should be **moist, well drained, slightly acidic** and **organically rich.**

This plant is considered self-cleaning because the petals fall cleanly from the plant once they've finished blooming.

Tips

Morden Fireglow will stand out among a variety of sun-loving plants, making it ideal for mixed beds and borders. Cut the stems while the flowers are still buds to extend the longevity of the cut flowers in bouquets.

Recommended

Rosa 'Morden Fireglow' is an upright shrub that bears double blossoms formed in loosely cupped sprays. The large, globular hips that form in fall remain on the plant well into the following spring.

Features: unique, deep scarlet red with orange early-summer flowers that repeat in fall; upright form **Height:** 2–4'
Spread: 24–36" **Hardiness:** zones 2b–8

Morden Snowbeauty

Parkland Shrub Rose

Morden Snowbeauty is the only white bloomer of the Parkland series. It is also one of the most recent series introductions, released in 1998. This extremely hardy specimen bears a large quantity of blooms in early summer, with intermittent flowers thereafter.

A heavy, second flush of blooms can be encouraged by a little deadheading and regular fertilizing.

Growing

Morden Snowbeauty is tolerant of partial shade but prefers **full sun. Well-drained** but **moist, slightly acidic, humus-rich** soil is best.

Tips

Planted en masse, these white roses look strikingly beautiful. Morden Snowbeauty is also ideal for borders or left as a prolific specimen. Its foliage is healthy, highly resistant to disease and requires very little care or maintenance.

Recommended

Rosa 'Morden Snowbeauty' bears rather large, semi-double clusters of flowers exposing bright yellow stamens. This low-spreading shrub is covered in shiny, dark green, healthy foliage.

Features: small stature; white blossoms emerge in early summer and again in fall
Height: 12–40" **Spread:** 18"–4'
Hardiness: zones 2b–8

Morden Sunrise

Parkland Shrub Rose

The 1999 introduction of Morden Sunrise was highly anticipated, and the public received it very well. It remains as popular today as it was in the year of its introduction.

Growing

Morden Sunrise prefers **full sun**. The soil should be **well drained** but **moist, slightly acidic** and **rich with organic matter**. Cooler temperatures cause the flower color to intensify, while hotter weather results in paler, softer tones.

Tips

This rose is ideal for borders and mixed beds or grown as a specimen. Morden Sunrise is a colorful addition to just about any garden setting.

Recommended

Rosa 'Morden Sunrise' is a compact shrub, formed by erect stems, dense foliage and semi-double flowers. The first yellow variety in the Parkland series, it has a clean and fresh look with blooms in tones of apricot and yellow, along with attractive, shiny, dark green leaves.

This rose, bred for harsh winters, also performs beautifully in areas with mild winters.

Features: compact size; lightly scented, apricot flowers that emerge in early summer and again in fall
Height: 24–30" **Spread:** 24–30"
Hardiness: zones 3–8

Red-Leafed Rose

Rosa glauca

This rose thrives where most plants could not survive. The starry, pink blossoms make a striking contrast to the violet-tinted foliage. The foliage sometimes appears to change color depending on the degree of sun exposure.

Red-leafed Rose is sought after by floral designers for its colorful, dainty foliage, which is perfect for floral arrangements.

Growing

Red-leafed rose tolerates shade but prefers **full sun**. Most soils are fine but **well-drained**, **moist**, **slightly acidic** soil is best. Keep this species under control with regular pruning, which will encourage new and colorful shoots.

Tips

Red-leafed rose makes an ideal hedge because of its vigorous nature and arching, thorny, purple stems. Its burgundy hips and maroon stems lend color to a stark winter landscape. It also makes a splendid specimen.

Recommended

Rosa glauca is extremely popular among rosarians and novice gardeners alike because it is so hardy and disease resistant. Its flowers are followed by clusters of small, rounded, dark red hips that remain on the shrub well into the following spring.

Features: tall, upright form; single, mauve-pink flowers with white centers emerge in late spring and continue to bloom until summer **Height:** 6–10' **Spread:** 5–6' **Hardiness:** zones 2–8

American Bittersweet

Celastrus

American bittersweet is a rough-and-tumble, low-maintenance vine with a wilder appearance than other plants in the Wisconsin and Minnesota landscape.

Growing

American bittersweet grows well in **full sun** but tolerates partial shade. It adapts to almost any well-drained soil. **Poor** soil is preferred, because rich soil can create a monster. American bittersweet needs little to no pruning.

Male and female flowers usually bloom on separate plants. For assured fruit production, in addition to regular watering, both males and females need to be planted close together.

Tips

American bittersweet is a great choice for the edge of a woodland garden or in naturalized areas. It quickly covers old trees, fences, arbors, trellises, posts and walls. It can mask piles of rubble and old tree stumps. It effectively controls erosion on hard-to-maintain slopes.

These vines can girdle the stems of young trees or shrubs, sometimes damaging or killing them.

C. scandens (above & below)

Recommended

C. scandens is a deciduous twining vine or sprawling groundcover with glossy, dark green foliage that turns bright yellow in fall. Small, undistinguished, yellow-green to whitish flowers bloom in late spring. The orange seeds are enclosed by bright red arils (seed cups). The male and female pair of '**Indian Brave**' and '**Indian Maid**' ('Indian Maiden') are hardier than the species.

Also called: staff vine **Features:** fast growth; decorative fruit; fall color **Height:** 20–30' **Spread:** 3–6' **Hardiness:** zones 2–8

Black-Eyed Susan Vine

Thunbergia

T. alata (above & below)

This adaptable African native is gaining increased popularity as gardeners continue to seek out attractive vining plants for walls, trellises, posts and arbors.

Growing

Black-eyed Susan vines do well in **full sun, partial shade** or **light shade**. Grow in **fertile, evenly moist, well-drained** soil that is high in **organic matter**.

Tips

Black-eyed Susan vines can be trained to twine up and around fences, walls, trees and shrubs. They are also attractive trailing down from the top of a rock garden or rock wall, or growing in mixed containers and hanging baskets.

These vines are perennials treated as annuals. They can be quite vigorous and may need to be trimmed back from time to time.

Recommended

T. alata is a vigorous, twining climber. It bears yellow flowers, often with dark centers, in summer and fall. Cultivars with large flowers in yellow, orange or white are available.

T. grandiflora (skyflower vine, blue trumpet vine) is less commonly available than *T. alata*. It tends to bloom late, in early to mid-fall. This twining climber bears stunning, pale violet-blue flowers.

The blooms are actually trumpet-shaped, with the dark centers forming a tube.

Features: twining habit; yellow, orange, violet-blue, creamy white, dark-centered flowers **Height:** 5' or more **Spread:** equal to height, if trained **Hardiness:** tender perennial treated as an annual

Clematis
Clematis

hank heaven for clematis! When a northern gardener needs a fast-growing, climbing vine that covers itself with large, beautiful blooms, no other plant better fits the bill.

Growing
Clematis plants prefer **full sun** but tolerate partial shade. The soil should be **fertile, humus rich, moist** and **well drained**. These plants are quite cold hardy but will fare best when protected from the winter wind. Add mulch around the base of the plant, or grow large-leaved plants in front, so the soil around the clematis roots stays cool. The rootball should be planted about 2" beneath the surface of the soil.

Tips
Clematis vines can climb up structures such as trellises, railings, fences and arbors. They can also be allowed to grow over shrubs and up trees, and can be used as groundcover.

C. 'Etoile Violette' (above), C. 'Gravetye Beauty' (below)

Recommended
There are many species, hybrids and cultivars of clematis. The flower forms, blooming times and sizes of the plants can vary. Check with your local garden center to see what is available.

Also called: virgin's bower **Features:** twining habit; blue, purple, pink, yellow, red, white, early- to late-summer flowers; decorative seedheads **Height:** 8–30' **Spread:** 2–4' **Hardiness:** zones 3–8

Climbing Hydrangea
Hydrangea

H. anomala subsp. *petiolaris* (above & below)

A mature climbing hydrangea can cover an entire wall, and with its dark, glossy leaves and delicate, lacy flowers, it is quite possibly one of the most stunning climbing plants available.

Growing

Hydrangeas grow well in **full sun** or **partial shade**. Shade or partial shade will reduce leaf and flower scorch in the hotter regions. The soil should be of **average to high fertility**, **humus rich**, **moist** and **well drained**. These plants perform best in cool, moist conditions.

Climbing hydrangea will produce the most flowers when it is exposed to some direct sunlight each day.

Tips

Climbing hydrangea climbs up trees, walls, fences, pergolas and arbors. It clings to walls by means of aerial roots, so needs no support, just a somewhat textured surface. It also grows over rocks, can be used as a groundcover and can be trained to form a small tree or shrub.

Recommended

H. anomala subsp. *petiolaris* (*H. petiolaris*) is a clinging vine with dark, glossy green leaves that sometimes turn an attractive yellow in fall. For more than a month in mid-summer the vine is covered with white, lacy-looking flowers, and the entire plant appears to be veiled in a lacy mist.

Features: white flowers; clinging habit; exfoliating bark **Height:** 50–80'
Spread: 50–80' **Hardiness:** zones 4–9

Cup-and-Saucer Vine
Cobaea

Cup-and-saucer vine is a vigorous climber native to Mexico that produces frilly, purple flowers from spring until frost.

Growing

Cup-and-saucer vine prefers **full sun**. The soil should be **moist, well drained** and of **average fertility**. This plant is fond of hot weather and will do best if planted in a sheltered site with southern exposure. Keep the vine well watered and avoid overfertilizing. Excess nitrogen causes vigorous growth but delays flowering. Set the seeds on edge when planting and barely cover them with soil.

Tips

This vine requires a sturdy support in order to climb, such as a trellis, arbor or chain-link fence. It uses grabbing hooks to climb so won't be able to grow up a wall without something to grab. It can be trained to fill almost any space. In hanging baskets the vines will climb the hanger and spill over the edges.

These tender plants can be cut back a bit in fall and overwintered indoors.

C. scandens (above & below)

Recommended

C. scandens is a vigorous climbing vine with flowers that are creamy green when they open and mature to deep purple. Var. *alba* has white flowers.

Also called: cathedral bells **Features:** purple or white flowers; clinging habit; long blooming period **Height:** 6–25' **Spread:** equal to height, if trained **Hardiness:** tender perennial; treated as an annual

Grape
Vitis

The grape vine's bold foliage and colorful fruit provide a look of maturity to a garden and a feel of permanence and weight that many new gardens need.

Growing

Grapes require **full sun** in a warm, south-facing location. The soil should be **deep, moist** and **acidic**. Choose a location that warms quickly in spring. Grape vines need to be pruned and trained on an annual basis for the best fruit production and to keep the plants tidy. Winter protection is often required. Grapes are sensitive to an assortment of herbicides.

Tips

Grape vines can be trained to grow on almost any sturdy structure. They may need to be tied in place until the basic structure is established.

Recommended

V. 'Bluebell' is a cold-hardy, early-ripening, disease-resistant variety that bears sweet, juicy, good quality blue grapes.

V. 'Edelweiss' is a robust, early-ripening plant that bears large clusters of white grapes. Take care when tying and untying the fragile, young branches. (Zone 4–9)

V. 'Frontenac' is the hardiest red-fruited grape vine in Minnesota and Wisconsin. It is disease resistant. (Zone 4–9)

V. 'La Crescent' is a cold-hardy grape cultivar that bears white fruit. (Zones 3b–9)

V. 'Swenson Red' produces good quality grapes that store well. (Zone 5–9)

Features: edible fruit; summer foliage; long-lived; woody, climbing, deciduous vine
Height: 10–20' **Spread:** 10–20'
Hardiness: zones 3–9

Honeysuckle
Lonicera

The colorful, tropical-looking, often-fragrant blooms of *Lonicera* are reason enough to grow these popular, long-lived vines.

Growing
Honeysuckles grow well in **full sun** but tolerate partial shade. The soil should be **average to fertile, humus rich, moist** and **well drained**.

Tips
Honeysuckle vines are twining, deciduous climbers that can be trained to grow up a trellis, fence, arbor or other structure. They can spread as widely as they climb to fill the space provided.

Recommended
L. × *brownii* (scarlet trumpet honeysuckle, Brown's honeysuckle) bears red or orange flowers (zones 5–8). '**Dropmore Scarlet**' bears bright red flowers and is hardy to zone 4.

L. × *heckrottii* (goldflame honeysuckle) is a deciduous to semi-evergreen vine with attractive blue-green foliage. It bears fragrant, pink or yellow flowers. (Zones 4–8)

Choosing the right honeysuckle, planting it in the proper site and pruning regularly make all the difference in enjoying these plants.

L. × *brownii* 'Dropmore Scarlet' (above & below)

L. hirsuta (hairy honeysuckle, yellow honeysuckle) is a twining, climbing, hairy vine that has dull, dark green foliage, small clusters of yellow to orange flowers and red fruit. (Zones 3–8)

L. sempervirens (trumpet honeysuckle, coral honeysuckle) bears orange or red flowers. Many cultivars are available, with flowers in yellow, red or scarlet. (Zones 4–8)

Features: orange, red, yellow, pink, spring, summer or fall flowers; twining habit; fruit **Height:** 10–20' **Spread:** 10–20' **Hardiness:** zones 3–8

Kiwi

Actinidia

A. arguta 'Ananasaya' (above), A. arguta (below)

Kiwis are useful, vigorous and cold-hardy vining shrubs. No better choice exists for covering fences, trellises and pergolas in partial shade.

Both a male and a female vine must be present for fruit to be produced. The plants are often sold in pairs.

Growing

Kiwi vines grow best in **full sun**, but they also grow well in **partial shade**. The soil should be **fertile** and **well drained**. These plants require shelter from strong winds.

Tips

These vines need a sturdy structure to twine around. Pergolas, arbors and sufficiently large and sturdy fences provide good support. Given a trellis against a wall, a tree or some other upright structure, kiwis will twine upward all summer. They can also be grown in containers.

Kiwi vines can grow uncontrollably. Don't be afraid to prune them back if they get out of hand.

Recommended

All species listed here have fragrant, white flowers and small, smooth-skinned, yellowish green fruit.

A. arguta (hardy kiwi, bower actinidia) has dark green, heart-shaped leaves.

A. kolomikta (variegated kiwi vine, kolomikta actinidia) has green leaves strongly variegated with pink and white. (Zones 4–8)

A. polygama (silver vine) bears dark green foliage that has silver-white markings on the leaf tips or entire upper leaf surface. (Zones 4–8)

Features: white early-summer flowers; edible fruit; twining habit
Height: 15–30' **Spread:** indefinite
Hardiness: zones 3–8

Morning Glory
Ipomoea

I. alba (above), *I. tricolor* (below)

One of the most beautiful of all vining and climbing plants, morning glory has maintained its popularity for centuries.

Growing
Morning glory grows best in **full sun** in **light, well-drained** soil of **poor fertility** but tolerates any type of soil. Soak the seeds for 24 hours before sowing. Start seeds in individual peat pots if sowing indoors. Plant in late spring.

Tips
Morning glory can be grown anywhere: on fences, walls, trees, trellises or arbors. As a groundcover, it will cover any obstacle it encounters.

This vine must twine around objects, such as wire or twine, in order to climb. However, wide fence posts, walls or other broad objects are too large.

Recommended
I. alba (moonflower) has sweetly scented, white flowers that open at night.

I. lobata (mina lobata, firecracker vine, exotic love) has red buds and orange flowers that mature to yellow, giving the flower spike a fire-like appearance.

I. purpurea (common morning glory) bears trumpet-shaped flowers in purple, blue, pink or white.

I. tricolor (morning glory) produces purple or blue flowers with white centers. Many cultivars are available.

Features: fast growth; large, white, blue, pink, red, yellow, orange, purple, sometimes bicolored flowers; easy to grow **Height:** 10–15' **Spread:** 12–24" **Hardiness:** annual

Passion Flower
Passiflora

P. caerulea (above & below)

Many Biblical references are associated with this truly exotic vine. The blooms are spectacular, sometimes coming in bicolored or tricolored varieties.

Growing
Grow passion flower in **full sun** or **partial shade**. This plant prefers **well-drained, moist** soil of **average fertility**. Keep it **sheltered** from wind and cold. Plant out several weeks after the last frost.

Tips
Passion flower is a popular addition to mixed containers and makes an unusual focal point near a door or other entryway.

Many garden centers now sell small passion flower plants in spring. They will quickly climb trellises and other supports over the summer. Passion flower can be composted at the end of summer or cut back and brought inside to enjoy in a bright room over the winter.

The small round fruits are edible but not very tasty.

Recommended
P. caerulea (blue passion flower) bears unusual, purple-banded, purple-white flowers all summer. '**Constance Elliott**' bears fragrant, white flowers.

Fertilize passion flower sparingly. Too much nitrogen will encourage a lot of foliage but few flowers.

Features: exotic purple and white flowers; habit; foliage **Height:** up to 30'
Spread: variable **Hardiness:** zones 6–8

Sweet Pea
Lathyrus

The delicate flowers of this old-fashioned favorite float like butterflies throughout the pleasant foliage, making sweat pea one of America's favorite climbing plants.

Growing

Sweet pea prefers **full sun** but tolerates light shade. The soil should be **fertile**, high in **organic matter, moist** and **well drained**. Fertilize very lightly with a low-nitrogen fertilizer during the flowering season. This plant tolerates light frost. Deadhead all blooms.

Soak seeds in water for 24 hours, or nick them with a nail file before planting them. Planting a second crop of sweet pea about a month after the first one will ensure a longer blooming period.

Tips

Sweet peas will grow up poles, trellises and fences or over rocks. They cling by wrapping tendrils around whatever they are growing up. Use the low-growing, shrubby varieties in beds, borders and containers.

Recommended

There are many cultivars of *L. odoratus*, including some that are small and bushy rather than climbing. Heritage varieties are often the most fragrant.

L. odoratus cultivars (above & below)

Avoid planting sweet peas in the same location two years in a row to help prevent some diseases from occurring.

Features: clinging habit; pink, red, purple, lavender, blue, salmon, pale yellow, peach, white, bicolored summer flowers **Height:** 12"–6' **Spread:** 6–18" **Hardiness:** hardy annual

Trumpet Creeper
Campsis

C. radicans (above), C. × tagliabuana (below)

Trumpet creeper is a chugging locomotive of a plant that will cover, entwine and ascend anything and everything in its path.

Growing

These heat-tolerant vines grow well in full sun, partial shade or light shade but flower best in **full sun**. They will grow in any soil, but growth is most rampant in **fertile** soil.

Tips

Trumpet creepers cling to any surface—a wall, a tree, a fence or a telephone pole. Once you have one of these vines, you will probably never get rid of it. One plant can provide a privacy screen very quickly, or it can be grown up an exterior wall or over the porch of a house. Trumpet creepers can be used on arbors and trellises but need frequent pruning to stay attractive and within bounds.

Recommended

C. radicans is a fast-growing, deciduous vine that bears dark orange, trumpet-shaped flowers for a long period in summer. 'Crimson Trumpet' has bright red flowers. 'Flava' bears yellow flowers.

C. × tagliabuana INDIAN SUMMER ('Kudian') grows to 10–13' tall and wide, producing prominently veined, light salmon-orange flowers with darker orange-red throats throughout summer. (Zones 4–8)

Hummingbirds are attracted to the long, tube-like flowers of trumpet creepers.

Also called: trumpet vine **Features:** clinging habit; orange, red, yellow summer flowers **Height:** 10–60' **Spread:** 10–60' **Hardiness:** zones 4–9

Virginia Creeper & Boston Ivy

Parthenocissus

P. quinquefolia (above & below)

Virginia creeper and Boston ivy are handsome vines that establish quickly and provide an air of age and permanence, even on new structures.

Growing

These vines grow well in any light from **full sun to full shade**. The soil should be **fertile** and **well drained**. The plants adapt to clay or sandy soils.

Virginia creeper can cover the sides of buildings and helps keep them cool in the summer heat. Cut the plants back to keep windows and doors accessible.

Tips

Virginia creeper and Boston ivy can cover an entire building, given enough time. They do not require support because they have clinging rootlets that can adhere to just about any surface, even smooth wood, vinyl, glass, or metal. Give the plants a lot of space and let them cover a wall, fence or arbor. When used as groundcovers, they will spread 50' but will be only 1' tall.

Recommended

P. quinquefolia (Virginia creeper, woodbine) has dark green foliage. Each leaf, divided into five leaflets, turns flame red in fall. 'Engelmanii' (var. *engelmanii*) clings better and spreads less rapidly than the species.

P. tricuspidata (Boston ivy, Japanese creeper) has dark green, three-lobed leaves that turn red in fall. This species is hardy to zone 4.

Features: summer and fall foliage; clinging habit
Height: 1–70' **Spread:** 30–70' **Hardiness:** zones 3–9

Canna Lily
Canna

Canna lilies are stunning, dramatic plants that add an exotic flair to any garden.

Growing

Canna lilies grow best in **full sun** in a **sheltered** location. The soil should be **fertile, moist** and **well drained**. Plant out in spring, once soil has warmed. Plants can be started early indoors in containers to get a head start on the growing season. Deadhead to prolong blooming.

The rhizomes can be lifted after the foliage is killed back in fall. Clean off any clinging dirt and store them in a cool, frost-free location in slightly moist peat moss. Check on them regularly through the winter and if they are starting to sprout, pot them and move them to a bright window until they can be moved outdoors.

Tips

Canna lilies can be grown in a bed or border. They make dramatic specimen plants and can even be included in large planters.

Recommended

A wide range of canna lilies are available, including cultivars and hybrids with green, bronzy, purple or yellow-and-green-striped foliage. Flowers may be white, red, orange, pink, yellow or bicolored. Dwarf cultivars that grow 18–28" tall are also available.

C. 'Red King Humbert' (above & below)

Features: decorative foliage, white, red, orange, pink, yellow, bicolored summer flowers **Height:** 3–6' **Spread:** 20–36" **Hardiness:** zones 7–8; grown as an annual

Crocus

Crocus

C. × *vernus* cultivars (above & below)

Crocuses are harbingers of spring. They often appear, as if by magic, in full bloom from beneath the melting snow.

Growing

Crocuses grow well in **full sun** or **light, dappled shade**. The soil should be of **poor to average fertility, gritty** and **well drained**. The corms are planted about 4" deep in fall.

Tips

Crocuses are almost always planted in groups. Drifts of crocuses can be planted in lawns to provide interest and color while the grass still lies dormant. In beds and borders they can be left to naturalize. Groups of plants will fill in and spread out to provide a bright welcome in spring.

Recommended

Many crocus species, hybrids and cultivars are available. The spring-flowering crocus most people are familiar with is **C. × *vernus***, commonly called Dutch crocus. Many cultivars are available with flowers in shades of purple, yellow, white, sometimes bicolored or with darker veins.

Saffron is obtained from the dried, crushed stigmas of C. sativus. Six plants produce enough spice for one recipe. This fall-blooming plant is hardy to zone 6.

Features: purple, yellow, white, sometimes bicolored, early-spring flowers **Height:** 2–6" **Spread:** 2–4" **Hardiness:** zones 3–8

Daffodil

Narcissus

Many gardeners automatically think of large, yellow, trumpet-shaped flowers when they think of daffodils, but there is a lot of variety in flower color, form and size among the daffodils.

The cup in the center of a daffodil is called the corona, and the group of petals that surrounds the corona is called the perianth.

Growing

Daffodils grow best in **full sun** or **light, dappled shade**. The soil should be **average to fertile, moist** and **well drained**. Bulbs should be planted in fall, 2–8" deep, depending on the size of the bulb. The bigger the bulb the deeper it should be planted. A rule of thumb is to measure the bulb from top to bottom and multiply that number by three to know how deep to plant.

Tips

Daffodils are often planted, where they can be left to naturalize, in the light shade beneath a tree or in a woodland garden. In mixed beds and borders, the faded leaves are hidden by the summer foliage of other plants.

Recommended

Many species, hybrids and cultivars of daffodils are available. Flowers come in shades of white, yellow, peach, orange, pink or may be bicolored. Flowers may be 1$\frac{1}{2}$–6" across, solitary or borne in clusters. There are 12 flower form categories.

Features: white, yellow, peach, orange, pink, bicolored spring flowers **Height:** 4–24" **Spread:** 4–12"
Hardiness: zones 3–8

Dahlia

Dahlia

Be careful as you delve in the world of dahlias—some gardeners become so bewitched by their wide array of magnificent flowers that they plant and grow little else.

Growing

Dahlias prefer **full sun**. The soil should be **fertile, rich in organic matter, moist** and **well drained**. Tubers can be purchased and started early indoors. The tubers can also be lifted in fall and stored over winter in slightly moist peat moss. Pot them and keep them in a bright room when they start sprouting in mid- to late winter. Deadhead to keep plants tidy and blooming.

Tips

Dahlias make attractive, colorful additions to a mixed border. The smaller varieties make good edging plants and the larger ones make good alternatives to shrubs. Varieties with unusual or interesting flowers are attractive specimen plants.

Recommended

Of the many dahlia hybrids, most are grown from tubers but a few can be started from seed. Many hybrids are sold based on flower shape, such as collarette, decorative or peony-flowered. The flowers range in size from 2–12" and are available in shades of purple, pink, white, yellow, orange or red with some bicolored.

Dahlias prefer cooler conditions, so the days of late summer and autumn bring out the best show of color.

Features: purple, pink, white, yellow, orange, red, bicolored summer flowers; attractive foliage; bushy habit **Height:** 8"–5' **Spread:** 8–18" **Hardiness:** tender tuberous perennial; grown as an annual

Flowering Onion
Allium

A. giganteum (above), A. cernuum (below)

Although the leaves have an onion scent when bruised, the flowers are often sweetly fragrant.

*F*lowering onions, with their striking, ball-like or loose, nodding clusters of flowers, are sure to attract attention in the garden.

Growing

Flowering onions grow best in **full sun**. The soil should be **average to fertile, moist** and **well drained**. Plant bulbs in fall, 2–4" deep, depending on size of bulb.

Tips

Flowering onions are best planted in groups in a bed or border where they can be left to naturalize. Most will self-seed when left to their own devices. The foliage, which tends to fade just as the plants come into flower, can be hidden with groundcover or a low, bushy companion plant.

Recommended

Several flowering onion species, hybrids and cultivars have gained popularity for their decorative, pink, purple, white, yellow, blue or maroon flowers. These include *A. aflatunense*, with dense, globe-like clusters of lavender flowers; *A. caeruleum* (blue globe onion), with globe-like clusters of blue flowers; *A. cernuum* (nodding or wild onion), with loose, drooping clusters of pink flowers; and *A. giganteum* (giant onion), a big plant that grows up to 6' tall, with large, globe-shaped clusters of pinky purple flowers.

Features: blue, purple, pinkish summer flowers; cylindrical or strap-shaped leaves
Height: 12"–6' **Spread:** 2–12"
Hardiness: zones 3–8

Gladiolus
Gladiolus

Perhaps best known as a cut flower, gladiolus adds an air of extravagance to the garden.

Growing

Gladiolus grows best in **full sun** but tolerates partial shade. The soil should be **fertile, humus rich, moist** and **well drained**. Flower spikes may need staking and a **sheltered** location out of the wind to prevent the flower spike from blowing over.

Plant corms in spring, 4–6" deep, once soil has warmed. Corms can also be started early indoors. Plant a few corms each week for about a month to prolong the blooming period.

Tips

Planted in groups in beds and borders, gladiolus makes a bold statement. Corms should be dug up in fall and stored in damp peat moss in a cool, frost-free location for the winter. If left in the ground over winter in USDA zones 2–4, the plants will quickly die out.

Recommended

G. × hortulanus is a huge group of hybrids. Gladiolus flowers come in almost every imaginable shade, except blue. Plants are commonly grouped in three classifications: **Grandiflorus** is the best known, each corm producing a single spike of large, often-ruffled flowers; **Nanus**, the hardiest group, survives

G. × *hortulanus* Grandiflorus (above), G. 'Homecoming' (below)

in zone 3 with protection and produces several spikes of up to seven flowers; and **Primulinus** produces a single spike of up to 23 flowers that grow more spaced out than those of the grandiflorus.

Over 10,000 cultivars of gladiolus have been developed.

Features: brightly colored mid- to late-summer flowers **Height:** 18"–6' **Spread:** 6–12" **Hardiness:** zone 8; grown as an annual

Lily

Lilium

L. Oriental Hybrids (above), *L.* 'Stargazer' (below)

ecorative clusters of large, richly colored blooms grace these tall plants. Flowers are produced at differing times of the season, depending on the hybrid, so it is possible to have lilies blooming all season if a variety of cultivars are chosen.

Growing

Lilies grow best in **full sun** but like to have their **roots shaded**. The soil should be rich in **organic matter, fertile, moist** and **well drained**.

Lily bulbs should be planted in fall before the first frost but can also be planted in spring if bulbs are available.

Tips

Lilies are often grouped in beds and borders and can be naturalized in woodland gardens and near water features. These plants are narrow and tall; plant at least three plants together to create some volume.

Recommended

The many species, hybrids and cultivars available are grouped by type. Visit your local garden center to see what is available. The following are two popular groups of lilies: **Asiatic Hybrids** bear clusters of flowers in early or mid-summer and are available in a wide range of colors; **Oriental Hybrids** bear clusters of large, fragrant flowers in mid- and late summer. Colors are usually white, pink or red.

Also called: oriental lily **Features:** early-, mid- or late-season flowers in shades of orange, yellow, peach, pink, purple, red, white **Height:** 2–5' **Spread:** 12" **Hardiness:** zones 4–8

Tulip
Tulipa

T. hybrids (above & below)

Tulips, with their beautiful, often garishly colored flowers are a welcome sight as we enjoy the warm days of spring.

Growing

Tulips grow best in **full sun**. In light or partial shade the flowers tend to bend toward the light. The soil should be **fertile** and **well drained**. Plant bulbs in fall, 4–6" deep, depending on size of bulb. Bulbs that have been cold-treated can be planted in spring. Although tulips can repeat bloom, many hybrids perform best if planted new each year.

During the tulipomania of the 1630s, the bulbs were worth many times their weight in gold, and many tulip speculators lost massive fortunes when the mania ended.

Tips

Tulips provide the best display when mass planted or planted in groups in flowerbeds and borders. They can also be grown in containers and can be forced to bloom early in indoor pots. Some of the species and older cultivars can be naturalized in meadow and wildflower gardens.

Recommended

There are about 100 species of tulips and thousands of hybrids and cultivars. They are generally divided into 15 groups based on bloom time and flower appearance. They come in dozens of shades, with many bicolored or multi-colored varieties. Blue is the only shade not available. Check with your local garden center in early fall for the best selection.

Features: colorful spring flowers **Height:** 6–30"
Spread: 2–8" **Hardiness:** zones 3–8; often treated as an annual

Basil
Ocimum

The sweet, fragrant leaves of fresh basil add a delicious licorice-like flavor to salads and tomato-based dishes.

Growing
Basil grows best in a **warm, sheltered** location in **full sun**. The soil should be **fertile, moist** and **well drained**. Pinch tips regularly to encourage bushy growth. Plant out or direct sow seed after frost danger has passed in spring.

Tips
Although basil grows best in a warm spot outdoors in the garden, it can be grown successfully indoors in a pot by a bright window to provide you with fresh leaves all year.

Recommended
O. basilicum is one of the most popular of the culinary herbs. There are dozens of varieties, including ones with large or tiny, green or purple and smooth or ruffled leaves.

O. basilicum 'Genovese' (above & below)

Basil is a good companion plant for tomatoes—both like warm, moist growing conditions and when you pick tomatoes for a salad you'll also remember to include a few sprigs or leaves of basil.

Features: fragrant, decorative leaves
Height: 12–24" **Spread:** 12–18"
Hardiness: tender annual

Chives

Allium

The delicate onion flavor of chives is best enjoyed fresh. Mix chives into dips or sprinkle them on salads and baked potatoes.

Growing

Chives grow best in **full sun**. The soil should be **fertile, moist** and **well drained**, but chives adapt to most soil conditions. These plants are easy to start from seed, but they do like the soil temperature to stay above 66° F before they will germinate, so seeds started directly in the garden are unlikely to sprout before early summer.

Tips

Chives are decorative enough to be included in a mixed or herbaceous border and can be left to naturalize. In an herb garden, chives should be given plenty of space to allow self-seeding.

Recommended

A. schoenoprasum forms a clump of bright green, cylindrical leaves. Clusters of pinky purple flowers are produced in early and mid-summer. Varieties with white or pink flowers are available.

Features: foliage; form; pinkish purple flowers **Height:** 8–24" **Spread:** 12" or more **Hardiness:** zones 3–8

A. schoenoprasum (above & below)

Chives will spread with reckless abandon as the clumps grow larger and the plants self-seed.

Chives are said to increase appetite and encourage good digestion.

Coriander • Cilantro
Coriandrum

C. sativum (above & below)

Coriander is a multi-purpose herb. The leaves, called cilantro and used in salads, salsas and soups, and the seeds, called coriander and used in pies, chutneys and marmalades, have distinct flavors and culinary uses.

Growing
Coriander prefers **full sun** but tolerates partial shade. The soil should be **fertile, light** and **well drained**. These plants dislike humid conditions and do best during a dry summer.

Tips
Coriander has pungent leaves and is best planted where people will not have to brush past it. It is, however, a delight to behold when in flower. Add a plant or two here and there throughout your borders and vegetable garden, both for the visual appeal and to attract beneficial insects.

Recommended
C. sativum forms a clump of lacy basal foliage above which large, loose clusters of tiny, white flowers are produced. The seeds ripen in late summer and fall.

The delicate, cloud-like clusters of flowers attract pollinating insects such as butterflies and bees, as well as abundant predatory insects that help keep pest insects to a minimum.

Also called: cilantro **Features:** form; foliage; white flowers; seeds **Height:** 16–24"
Spread: 8–16" **Hardiness:** tender annual

Dill
Anethum

Dill leaves and seeds are probably best known for their use as pickling herbs, though they have a wide variety of other culinary uses.

Growing

Dill grows best in **full sun** in a **sheltered** location out of strong winds. The soil should be of **poor to average fertility, moist** and **well drained**. Sow seeds every couple of weeks in spring and early summer to ensure a regular supply of leaves. Plants should not be grown near fennel because the plants will cross-pollinate and the seeds will lose their distinct flavors.

Tips

With its feathery leaves, dill is an attractive addition to a mixed bed or border. It can be included in a vegetable garden but does well in any sunny location. It also attracts predatory insects.

Recommended

A. graveolens forms a clump of feathery foliage. Clusters of yellow flowers are borne at the tops of sturdy stems.

A popular Scandinavian dish called gravalax *is made by marinating a fillet of salmon with the leaves and seeds of dill.*

Features: feathery, edible foliage; yellow summer flowers; edible seeds
Height: 2–5' **Spread:** 12" or more
Hardiness: annual

A. graveolens (above & below)

Mint
Mentha

M. × piperata 'Chocolate' (above), M. × gracilis 'Variegata' (below)

A few sprigs of fresh mint added to a pitcher of iced tea give it an added zip.

The cool, refreshing flavor of mint lends itself to tea and other hot or cold beverages. Mint sauce, made from freshly chopped leaves, is often served with lamb.

Growing
Mint grows well in **full sun** or **partial shade**. The soil should be **average to fertile, humus rich** and **moist**. These plants spread vigorously by rhizomes and may need a barrier in the soil to restrict their spread.

Tips
Mint is a good groundcover for damp spots. It grows well along ditches that may only be periodically wet. It also can be used in beds and borders but may overwhelm less vigorous plants.

The flowers attract bees, butterflies and other pollinators to the garden.

Recommended
There are many species, hybrids and cultivars of mint. **Spearmint** (*M. spicata*), **peppermint** (*M. × piperita*) and **orange mint** (*M. × piperata* var. *citrata*) are three of the most commonly grown culinary varieties. There are also more decorative varieties with variegated or curly leaves, as well as varieties with unusual, fruit-scented leaves.

Features: fragrant foliage; purple, pink, white summer flowers **Height:** 6–36" **Spread:** 36" or more **Hardiness:** zones 4–8

Oregano • Marjoram

Origanum

Oregano and marjoram are two of the best known and most frequently used herbs. They are popular in stuffings, soups and stews, and no pizza is complete until it has been sprinkled with fresh or dried oregano leaves.

Growing

Oregano and marjoram grow best in **full sun**. The soil should be of **poor to average fertility, neutral to alkaline** and **well drained**. The flowers attract pollinators to the garden.

Tips

These bushy perennials make a lovely addition to any border and can be trimmed to form low hedges.

Recommended

O. majorana (marjoram) is upright and shrubby with light green, hairy leaves. It bears white or pink flowers in summer and can be grown as an annual where it is not hardy.

O. vulgare subsp. *hirtum* (oregano, Greek oregano) is the most flavorful culinary variety of oregano. This low, bushy plant has hairy, gray-green leaves and bears white flowers. Many other interesting varieties of *O. vulgare* are available, including those with golden, variegated or curly leaves.

O. vulgare 'Aureum' (above & below)

In Greek, oros *means 'mountain,' and* ganos *means 'joy and beauty,' so* oregano *translates as 'joy or beauty of the mountain.'*

Features: fragrant foliage; white or pink summer flowers; bushy habit **Height:** 12–32"
Spread: 8–18" **Hardiness:** zones 5–8

Parsley
Petroselinum

P. crispum (above), P. crispum var. crispum (below)

Although usually used as a garnish, parsley is rich in vitamins and minerals and is reputed to freshen the breath after garlic- or onion-rich foods are eaten.

Parsley leaves make a tasty and nutritious addition to salads. Tear freshly picked leaves and sprinkle them over or mix them in your mixed greens.

Growing

Parsley grows well in **full sun** or **partial shade**. The soil should be of **average to rich fertility, humus rich, moist** and **well drained**. Direct sow seeds because the plants resent transplanting. If you start seeds early, use peat pots so the plants can be potted or planted out without disruption.

Tips

Parsley should be started where you mean to grow it. Containers of parsley can be kept close to the house for easy picking. The bright green leaves and compact growth habit make parsley a good edging plant for beds and borders.

Recommended

P. crispum forms a clump of bright green, divided leaves. This plant is biennial but is usually grown as an annual. Cultivars may have flat or curly leaves. Flat leaves are more flavorful and curly are more decorative. Dwarf cultivars are also available.

Features: attractive foliage **Height:** 8–24"
Spread: 12–24" **Hardiness:** zones 5–8; grown as an annual

Rosemary

Rosmarinus

*T*he needle-like leaves of rosemary are used to flavor a wide variety of culinary dishes, including chicken, pork, lamb, rice, tomato and egg dishes.

Growing

Rosemary prefers **full sun** but tolerates partial shade. The soil should be of **poor to average fertility** and **well drained.**

Tips

Rosemary is often grown in a shrub border where hardy. Try growing it in a container as a specimen or with other plants. Low-growing, spreading plants can be included in a rock garden, grown along the top of a retaining wall or grown in hanging baskets.

Recommended

R. officinalis is a dense, bushy, evergreen shrub with narrow, dark green leaves. The habit varies somewhat between cultivars from strongly upright to prostrate and spreading. Flowers are usually in shades of blue, but pink-flowered cultivars are available. Plants rarely reach their mature size when grown in containers.

R. officinalis (above & below)

To overwinter a container-grown plant, keep it in very light or partial shade in summer, then put it in a sunny window indoors for winter and keep it well watered, but not soaking wet.

Features: fragrant, evergreen foliage; bright blue, sometimes pink, summer flowers **Height:** 8"–4'
Spread: 1–4' **Hardiness:** zone 8; grown as an annual

Sage

Salvia

S. officinalis 'Icterina' (above), S. officinalis 'Purpurescens' (below)

Sage has been used since at least ancient Greek times as a medicinal and culinary herb and continues to be widely used for both those purposes today.

Sage is perhaps best known as a flavoring for stuffing, but it has a great range of uses, including in soups, stews, sausages and dumplings.

Growing

Sage prefers **full sun** but tolerates light shade. The soil should be of **average fertility** and **well drained**. These plants benefit from a light mulch of compost each year. They are drought tolerant once established.

Tips

Sage is an attractive plant for borders; it can be used to add volume to the middle, or as an attractive edging or feature plant near the front. Sage can also be grown in mixed planters.

Recommended

S. officinalis is a woody, mounding plant with soft, gray-green leaves. Spikes of light purple flowers appear in early and mid-summer. Many cultivars with attractive foliage are available, including the silver-leaved 'Berggarten'; the yellow-margined 'Icterina'; the purple-leaved 'Purpurea'; and the purple-green and cream variegated 'Tricolor,' which has a pink flush to the new growth.

Features: fragrant decorative foliage; blue or purple summer flowers **Height:** 12–24"
Spread: 18–36"
Hardiness: zones 4–7

Thyme

Thymus

Thyme will tell everyone entering your garden that you're at the forefront of fashionable gardening trends, for this petite perennial has left the herb jar and moved front and center as a highly valuable ornamental plant.

Growing

Thyme prefers **full sun**. The soil should be **neutral to alkaline** and of **poor to average fertility. Good drainage** is essential. It is beneficial to work leaf mold into the soil to improve structure and drainage.

Tips

Thyme is useful for sunny, dry locations at the front of borders, between or beside paving stones, on rock gardens and rock walls, and in containers.

Once the plants have finished flowering, shear them back by about half to encourage new growth and to prevent the plants from becoming too woody.

T. vulgaris (above), *T. × citriodorus* (below)

Recommended

T. × citriodorus (lemon-scented thyme) forms a mound of lemon-scented, dark green foliage. The flowers are pale pink. Cultivars with silver- or gold-margined leaves are available.

T. vulgaris (common thyme) forms a bushy mound of dark green leaves. The flowers may be purple, pink or white. Cultivars with variegated leaves are available.

These plants are bee magnets when blooming; thyme honey is pleasantly herbal and goes very well with biscuits.

Features: bushy habit; fragrant, decorative foliage; purple, pink, white flowers **Height:** 4–18"
Spread: 10–16" **Hardiness:** zones 4–8

Blue Fescue
Festuca

F. glauca 'Elijah Blue' (above), *F. glauca* (below)

This fine-leaved ornamental grass forms tufted clumps that resemble pincushions. Its metallic blue coloring adds an all-season cooling accent to the garden.

Growing

Blue fescue thrives in **full sun to light shade**. The soil should be of **average fertility, moist** and **well drained**. Plants are drought tolerant once established. Blue fescue emerges early in the spring, so shear it back to 1" above the crown in late winter before new growth emerges. Cut off flower stalks just above the foliage to keep the plant tidy or to prevent self-seeding.

Tips

With its fine texture and distinct blue color, this grass can be used as a single specimen in a rock garden or a container planting. Plant blue fescue in drifts to create a sea of blue, or a handsome edge to a bed, border or pathway. It looks attractive in both formal and informal gardens.

Recommended

F. ovina var. *glauca* forms tidy, tufted clumps of fine, blue-toned foliage and panicles of flowers in May and June. Cultivars and hybrids come in varying heights and in shades ranging from blue to olive green. **'Boulder Blue,' 'Elijah Blue,' 'Skinner's Blue'** and **'Solling'** are popular selections.

Also called: blue sheep fescue
Features: blue to blue-green foliage; color that persists into winter; habit **Height:** 6–12"
Spread: 10–12" **Hardiness:** zones 3–9

Brunnera

Brunnera

There are many wonderful shade plants suited perfectly to our northern climate, but brunnera happens to be one of the best.

Growing

Brunnera prefers **light shade** but tolerates morning sun with consistent moisture. The soil should be of **average fertility, humus rich, moist** and **well drained**. The species and its cultivars are not drought tolerant. Divide in spring when the center of the clump appears to be drying out.

Cut back faded foliage mid-season to produce a flush of new growth.

Tips

Brunnera makes a great addition to a woodland or shaded garden. Its low, bushy habit makes it useful as a groundcover or as an addition to a shaded border.

B. macrophyla cultivar (above), *B. macrophylla* 'Dawson's White' (below)

Recommended

B. macrophylla forms a mound of soft, heart-shaped leaves and produces loose clusters of clear blue flowers. **'Dawson's White'** ('Variegata') has large leaves with irregular, creamy patches. **'Hadspen Cream'** has leaves with creamy margins. Grow variegated plants in light or full shade to avoid scorched leaves. **'Langtrees'** has blue flowers and large leaves with silver spots.

Brunnera is a reliable plant that rarely suffers from any problems.

Also called: Siberian bugloss
Features: blue spring flowers; bold, attractive foliage; long lived **Height:** 12–18"
Spread: 18–24" **Hardiness:** zones 3–8

Flowering Fern
Osmunda

O. cinnamomea (above & below)

Ferns have a certain prehistoric mystique and can add a sculptural elegance and textural accent to the garden.

Growing

Flowering ferns prefer **full shade to light shade** but tolerate full sun if the soil is consistently moist. The soil should be **fertile, humus rich, acidic** and **moist**. Flowering ferns tolerate wet soil and will spread as offsets form at the plant bases.

Tips

These large ferns form an attractive mass when planted in large colonies. They can be included in beds and borders, and make a welcome addition to a woodland garden.

Recommended

O. cinnamomea (cinnamon fern) has light green fronds that fan out in a circular fashion from a central point. Bright green, leafless, fertile fronds that mature to cinnamon brown are produced in spring and stand straight up in the center of the plant.

O. regalis (royal fern) forms a dense clump of foliage. Feathery, flower-like, fertile fronds stand out among the sterile fronds in summer, and mature to a rusty brown. 'Purpurescens' fronds are purple-red when they emerge in spring and then mature to green. This contrasts well with the purple stems. (Zones 3–8)

The flowering fern's 'flowers' are actually its spore-producing sporangia.

Features: perennial, deciduous fern; decorative, fertile fronds; habit **Height:** 30"–5'
Spread: 24–36" **Hardiness:** zones 2–8

Fountain Grass

Pennisetum

 ountain grass's low maintenance and graceful
form make it easy to place. It
will soften any landscape, even
in winter.

Growing

Fountain grass thrives in **full sun**
in **well-drained** soil of **average
fertility**. Plants are drought
tolerant once established.
They may self-seed but are not
troublesome. Shear perennials
back in early spring, and divide
them when they start to die out
in the center.

Tips

Fountain grass can be used as
individual specimen plants or
in group plantings and drifts
or combined with flowering
annuals, perennials, shrubs
and other ornamental grasses.
Annual selections are often
planted in containers.

Recommended

Popular perennials include
P. alopecuroides 'Hameln'
(dwarf perennial fountain
grass), a compact cultivar
with silvery white plumes
and narrow, dark green foliage
that turns gold in fall.

The name Pennisetum *refers
to the plumy flower spikes.
In Latin,* penna *means feather,
and* seta *means bristle.*

P. setaceum 'Rubrum' (above & below)

Annuals include *P. glaucum* 'Purple Majesty'
(purple ornamental millet), which has blackish
purple foliage and coarse, bottlebrush flowers. Its
form resembles a corn stalk. *P. setaceum* (annual
fountain grass) has narrow, green foliage and pinkish purple flowers that mature to gray. **'Rubrum'**
(red annual fountain grass) has broader, deep
burgundy foliage and pinkish purple flowers.

Features: arching, fountain-like habit; silvery pink,
dusty rose to purplish black foliage; pinkish purple
flowers; winter interest **Height:** 2–5' **Spread:** 2–3'
Hardiness: zones 5–8 or grown as annual

Lungwort
Pulmonaria

P. saccharata (above & below)

Here's a highly useful shade plant that combines wonderfully with ferns, heucheras, hostas, and most other denizens of shady spaces. And while lovely in flower, this is a plant that brings fabulous foliage to the party.

Growing
Lungworts prefer **partial to full shade**. The soil should be **fertile, humus rich, moist** and **well drained**. Rot can occur in very wet soil.

Divide in early summer after flowering or in fall. Provide the newly planted divisions with a lot of water to help them re-establish. Deadhead to keep the plants tidy.

Tips
Lungworts make useful and attractive groundcovers for shady borders, woodland gardens and pond and stream edges.

Recommended
There are many excellent species, cultivars and hybrids offering tremendous choice in leaf size and coloration. Check with your local nursery or garden center to see what is available. The following are three popular species.

P. longifolia (long-leaved lungwort) is a dense plant with long, narrow, white-spotted, green leaves and clusters of blue flowers.

P. officinalis (common lungwort, spotted dog) forms a loose clump of evergreen foliage, spotted with white. The flowers open pink and mature to blue.

P. saccharata (Bethlehem sage) has large, white-spotted, evergreen leaves and purple, red or white flowers.

Features: decorative, mottled foliage; pink, red, white, blue, purple spring flowers **Height:** 8–24" **Spread:** 8–36" **Hardiness:** zones 3–8

Maidenhair Fern

Adiantum

A. pedatum (above & below)

These charming and delicate-looking native ferns add a graceful touch to any woodland planting. Their unique habit and texture really stand out.

Growing

Maidenhair fern grows well in **light shade** or **partial shade** but tolerates full shade. The soil should be of **average fertility, humus rich, slightly acidic** and **moist**. This plant rarely needs dividing, but it can be divided in spring to propagate more plants.

Tips

These lovely ferns will do well in any shaded spot. Include them in rock gardens, woodland gardens, shaded borders and beneath shade trees. They also make an attractive addition to a shaded planting next to a water feature or on a slope where the foliage can be seen when it sways in the breeze.

Recommended

A. pedatum forms a spreading mound of delicate, arching fronds. Light green leaflets stand out against the black stems, and the whole plant turns bright yellow in fall. Spores are produced on the undersides of the leaflets.

Try growing the fine-textured and delicate maidenhair fern with hosta, lungwort and brunnera. It will create a nice contrast in texture.

Also called: northern maidenhair fern
Features: deciduous perennial fern; summer and fall foliage; habit **Height:** 12–24"
Spread: 12–24" **Hardiness:** zones 2–8

Miscanthus

Miscanthus

M. sinensis cultivars (above & below)

Miscanthus is one of the most popular and majestic of all the ornamental grasses. Its graceful foliage dances in the wind and makes an impressive sight all year long.

Growing

Miscanthus prefers **full sun**. The soil should be of **average fertility, moist** and **well drained**, though some selections also tolerate wet soil. All selections are drought tolerant once established.

Tips

Give these magnificent beauties room to spread so you can fully appreciate their form. The plant's height will determine the best place for each selection in the border. They create dramatic impact in groups or as seasonal screens.

Recommended

There are many available cultivars of *M. sinensis*, all distinguished by the white midrib on the leaf blade. Some popular selections include '**Gracillimus**' (maiden grass), with long, fine-textured leaves; '**Grosse Fontaine**' (large fountain), a tall, wide-spreading, early-flowering selection; '**Morning Light**' (variegated maiden grass), a short and delicate plant with fine, white leaf edges; **var.** *purpurescens* (flame grass), with foliage that turns bright orange in early fall; and '**Strictus**' (porcupine grass), a tall, stiff, upright selection with unusual, horizontal, yellow bands.

Also called: eulalia, Japanese silver grass
Features: upright, arching habit; colorful summer and fall foliage; pink, copper, silver late-summer and fall flowers; winter interest **Height:** 4–8'
Spread: 2–4' **Hardiness:** zones 5–8, possibly zone 4

Ostrich Fern

Matteuccia

These popular, classic ferns are revered for their delicious, emerging spring fronds and their stately, vase-shaped habit.

Growing

Ostrich fern prefers **partial or light shade** but tolerates full shade and even full sun if the soil is kept moist. The soil should be **average to fertile, humus rich, neutral to acidic** and **moist**. Leaves may scorch if the soil is not moist enough.

These ferns are aggressive spreaders that reproduce by spores. Unwanted plants can be pulled up and composted or given away.

Tips

This fern appreciates a moist woodland garden and is often found growing wild alongside woodland streams and creeks. Useful in shaded borders, these plants are quick to spread, to the delight of those who enjoy the young fronds as a culinary delicacy.

Recommended

M. struthiopteris (*M. pennsylvanica*) forms a circular cluster of slightly arching, feathery fronds. Stiff, brown, fertile fronds, covered in reproductive spores, stick up in the center of the cluster in late summer and persist through winter. They are popular choices for dried arrangements.

Also called: fiddlehead fern
Features: perennial fern; foliage; habit
Height: 3–5' **Spread:** 12–36" or more
Hardiness: zones 1–8

M. struthiopteris (above & below)

Ostrich ferns are also grown commercially for their edible fiddleheads. The tightly coiled, new spring fronds taste delicious lightly steamed and served with butter. Remove the bitter, reddish brown, papery coating before steaming.

Pachysandra

Pachysandra

P. terminalis (above & below)

Pachysandra is a versatile, forgiving groundcover that looks great anywhere a low, dense mat of green is desired.

Growing

Pachysandras prefer **light to full shade** but tolerate partial shade. The soil should be **moist, humus rich** and **well drained**. Division is not required but can be done in spring for propagation.

These plants are evergreen and generally need little attention. Shearing back any winter damage in spring will quickly result in a flush of new growth.

To cover large areas, buy it in flats, then plant on a 12" grid. In just a few years you'll have a lush carpet, with ample plants to dig in the spring and move to other spots in the garden.

Tips

Pachysandras are durable groundcovers to use under trees, along north-facing walls, in shady borders and in woodland gardens. Allegheny spurge makes a nice accent plant in a naturalized, woodland setting.

Recommended

P. procumbens (Allegheny spurge, Allegheny pachysandra) is a spreading, clump-forming species that is hardy to zone 5. The semi-evergreen leaves emerge a light green, mature to bronze green and turn reddish in fall.

P. terminalis (Japanese spurge) forms a low mass of foliage rosettes. 'Variegata' has white margins or silver-mottled foliage. It is not as vigorous as the species.

Features: perennial, evergreen groundcover; habit; inconspicuous, fragrant, white spring flowers
Height: 8–12" **Spread:** indefinite
Hardiness: zones 4–9

Reed Grass

Calamagrostis

This is a graceful grass that changes its habit and flower color throughout the growing season. The slightest breeze keeps reed grass in perpetual motion.

Growing

Reed grass grows best in **full sun**. The soil should be **fertile, moist** and **well drained**, though heavy clay and dry soils are tolerated. Reed grass may be susceptible to rust in cool, wet summers or in areas with poor air circulation. Rain and heavy snow may cause it to flop temporarily, but it quickly bounces back. Cut reed grass back to 2–4" in very early spring before growth begins. Divide if it begins to die out in the center.

Tips

Whether it's used as a single, stately focal point in small groupings or in large drifts, this is a desirable, low-maintenance grass. It combines well with late-summer and fall-blooming perennials.

C. × *acutiflora* 'Karl Foerster' (above & below)

Recommended

C. x *acutiflora* '**Karl Foerster**' (Foerster's feather reed grass) forms a loose mound of green foliage from which airy, bottlebrush flowers emerge in June. The flowering stems have a loose, arching habit when they first emerge but grow stiffer and more upright over summer. Other cultivars include '**Overdam**,' a compact, less hardy selection with white leaf edges, and '**Avalanche**,' which has a white center stripe.

Features: open habit becomes upright; silvery pink flowers turn rich tan; green foliage turns bright gold in fall; winter interest **Height:** 3–5' **Spread:** 24–36" **Hardiness:** zones 4–9

Sweet Potato Vine
Ipomoea

I. batatas 'Margarita' (above & below)

Trailing varieties of sweet potato vine, with their compelling purple or lime green leaves, are outstanding in hanging baskets, window boxes and large containers.

Growing
Grow sweet potato vine in **full sun**. Any type of soil will do, but a **light, well-drained** soil of **poor fertility** is preferred.

As a bonus, when you pull up your plant at the end of summer, you can eat any tubers (sweet potatoes) that have formed.

Tips
Sweet potato vine is a great addition to mixed planters, window boxes and hanging baskets. In a rock garden it will scramble about, and along the top of a retaining wall it will cascade over the edge.

Recommended
I. batatas (sweet potato vine) is a twining climber that is grown for its attractive foliage rather than its flowers. Several cultivars are available. 'Black Heart' has heart-shaped, dark purple-green foliage with darker veins. 'Blackie' produces dark purple, deeply lobed leaves. 'Margarita' has heart-shaped, yellow-green foliage. 'Tricolor' has pink, green and white variegated foliage.

Features: decorative foliage **Height:** about 12" **Spread:** up to 10' **Hardiness:** tender tuberous perennial grown as an annual

Sweet Woodruff

Galium

G. odoratum (above & below)

Sweet woodruff is a groundcover with abundant good qualities: attractive, light green foliage that smells like new-mown hay; profuse, white spring flowers; and the ability to fill in garden spaces without taking over.

Growing

This plant prefers **partial shade**. It will grow well, but not bloom well, in full shade. The soil should be **humus rich**, **slightly acidic** and evenly **moist**. Sweet woodruff competes well with other plant roots and does well where some other groundcovers fail to thrive.

Sweet woodruff's vanilla-scented dried leaves and flowers were once used to scent bed linens and are often added to potpourri. They are also used to flavor beverages, particularly the traditional German May wine.

Tips

Sweet woodruff makes a perfect woodland groundcover. It forms a beautiful green carpet and loves the same conditions in which azaleas and rhododendrons thrive. Interplant it with spring bulbs for a fantastic display in spring.

Recommended

G. odoratum is a low, spreading groundcover. It bears clusters of star-shaped, white flowers in a flush in late spring, and these continue to appear sporadically through mid-summer.

Features: deciduous perennial groundcover; white late-spring to mid-summer flowers; fragrant foliage; habit **Height:** 12–18" **Spread:** indefinite **Hardiness:** zones 3–8

Switch Grass
Panicum

P. *virgatum* cultivar (above), P. *virgatum* 'Heavy Metal' (below)

A native to the prairie grasslands, switch grass naturalizes equally well in an informal border and a natural meadow.

Growing
Switch grass thrives in **full sun, light shade** or **partial shade** in **well-drained** soil of **average fertility.** Plants adapt to both moist and dry soils and tolerate conditions ranging from heavy clay to lighter, sandy soil. Cut switch grass back to 2–4" from the ground in early spring. The flower stems may break under heavy, wet snow or in exposed, windy sites.

Tips
Plant switch grass singly in small gardens, in large groups in spacious borders, or at the edges of ponds or pools for a dramatic effect. The seed-heads attract birds, and the foliage changes color in fall.

Recommended
P. virgatum (switch grass) is suited to wild meadow gardens. Some of its popular cultivars include '**Heavy Metal**' (blue switch grass), an upright plant with narrow, steely blue foliage flushed with gold and burgundy in fall; '**Prairie Sky**' (blue switch grass), an arching plant with deep blue foliage; and '**Shenandoah**' (red switch grass), with red-tinged, green foliage that turns burgundy in fall.

Switch grass's delicate, airy panicles fill gaps in the garden border and can be cut for fresh or dried arrangements.

Features: clumping habit; green, blue, burgundy foliage; airy panicles of flowers; fall color; winter interest **Height:** 3–5' **Spread:** 30–36" **Hardiness:** zones 3–8

Glossary

Acid soil: soil with a pH lower than 7.0

Annual: a plant that germinates, flowers, sets seed and dies in one growing season

Alkaline soil: soil with a pH higher than 7.0

Basal leaves: leaves that form from the crown, at the base of the plant

Bract: a modified leaf at the base of a flower or flower cluster

Corm: a bulb-like, food-storing, underground stem, resembling a bulb without scales

Crown: the part of the plant at or just below soil level where the shoots join the roots

Cultivar: a cultivated plant variety with one or more distinct differences from the species, e.g., in flower color or disease resistance

Damping off: fungal disease causing seedlings to rot at soil level and topple over

Deadhead: to remove spent flowers to maintain a neat appearance and encourage a longer blooming season

Direct sow: to sow seeds directly in the garden

Dormancy: a period of plant inactivity, usually during winter or unfavorable conditions

Double flower: a flower with an unusually large number of petals

Genus: a category of biological classification between the species and family levels; the first word in a scientific name indicates the genus

Grafting: a type of propagation in which a stem or bud of one plant is joined onto the rootstock of another plant of a closely related species

Hardy: capable of surviving unfavorable conditions, such as cold weather or frost, without protection

Hip: the fruit of a rose, containing the seeds

Humus: decomposed or decomposing organic material in the soil

Hybrid: a plant resulting from natural or human-induced cross-breeding between varieties, species or genera

Inflorescence: a flower cluster

Male clone: a plant that may or may not produce pollen but that will not produce fruit, seed or seedpods

Neutral soil: soil with a pH of 7.0

Perennial: a plant that takes three or more years to complete its life cycle

pH: a measure of acidity or alkalinity; the soil pH influences availability of nutrients for plants

Rhizome: a root-like, food-storing stem that grows horizontally at or just below soil level, from which new shoots may emerge

Rootball: the root mass and surrounding soil of a plant

Seedhead: dried, inedible fruit that contains seeds; the fruiting stage of the inflorescence

Self-seeding: reproducing by means of seeds without human assistance, so that new plants constantly replace those that die

Semi-double flower: a flower with petals in two or three rings

Single flower: a flower with a single ring of typically four or five petals

Species: the fundamental unit of biological classification; the entity from which cultivars and varieties are derived

Standard: a shrub or small tree grown with an erect main stem, accomplished either through pruning and training or by grafting the plant onto a tall, straight stock

Sucker: a shoot that comes up from the root, often some distance from the plant; it can be separated to form a new plant once it develops its own roots

Tender: incapable of surviving the climatic conditions of a given region and requiring protection from frost or cold

Tuber: the thick section of a rhizome bearing nodes and buds

Variegation: foliage that has more than one color, often patched or striped or bearing leaf margins of a different color

Variety: a naturally occurring variant of a species

Index

Entries in **bold** type indicate the main plant headings.

Abies, 84
Acer, 95
Achillea, 69
Actinidia, 134
  bower, 134
  kolomikta, 134
Adiantum, 163
Aesculus, 88
Ageratum, 11
Ajuga, 38
Alchemilla, 57
Alexander
  Mackenzie, 114
Allium (bulb), 144
Allium (herb), 149
Almond, 75
Alum root, 53
Amelanchier, 104
**American bitter-
  sweet**, 127
Anethum, 151
Antirrhinum, 33
Arborvitae, 70
  eastern, 70
  Russian, 103
Archangel, yellow,
  58
Aronia, 76
Arrowwood, 109
Artemisia, 39
  silvermound, 39
Aruncus, 51
Aspen, 100
  European
  columnar, 100
  Swedish
  columnar, 100
Aster, 40
  alpine, 40
  bushy, 40
  calico, 40
  heath, 40
  New England, 40

sky blue, 40
  smooth, 40
Astilbe, 41
  Arend's, 41
  Chinese, 41
  Japanese, 41
Azalea, 102
Balloon flower, 42
Barberry, 71
  Japanese, 71
Basil, 148
Basswood, 93
Beech, 72
  American, 72
  European, 72
Begonia, 12
  rex, 12
  tuberous, 12
  wax, 12
Belle Amour, 115
Bellflower, 46
  Carpathian, 46
  clustered, 46
  peach-leaved, 46
  Serbian, 46
Berberis, 71
Betula, 73
Birch, 73
  black, 73
  red, 73
  river, 73
**Black-eyed Susan
  (annual)**, 13
**Black-eyed Susan
  (perennial)**, 43
**Black-eyed Susan
  vine**, 128
**Blanc Double de
  Coubert**, 116
Blazing star, 59
  prairie, 59
  royal, 59
Blue fescue, 158

Blue trumpet vine,
  128
Boltonia, 44
Boneset, 56
  common, 56
Boston ivy, 139
Boxwood, 74
  Korean littleleaf,
  74
Browallia, 14
Brunnera, 159
Buckeye, 88
  bottlebrush, 88
  Ohio, 88
  red, 88
  yellow, 88
Bugbane, 45
  Kamchatka, 45
Buglewood, 38
Bugloss, Siberian,
  159
Burning bush, 82
Busy Lizzie, 24
Buxus, 74
Calamagrostis,
  167
Calendula, 15
Campanula, 46
Campsis, 138
Canna, 140
Canna lily, 140
Cathedral bells,
  131
Cedar, 70
  eastern white, 70
Celastrus, 127
Celosia, 16
  crested, 16
  plume, 16
  spicata, 16
  wheat, 16
Cercis, 101
Chamaecyparis, 83

Cherry, 75
Cherry pie plant,
  23
Chionanthus, 85
Chives, 149
Chokeberry, 76
  black, 76
  red, 76
Chrysanthemum,
  47
Cilantro, 150
Cimicifuga, 45
Clematis, 129
Cleome, 17
Clethra, 108
**Climbing
  hydrangea**, 130
Cobaea, 131
Cockscomb, 16
Cohosh, black, 45
Coleus, 18
**Coneflower
  (annual)**, 13
**Coneflower
  (echinacea)**, 48
  purple, 48
**Coneflower
  (perennial)**, 43
  cutleaf, 43
  shining, 43
Coral bells, 53
Coralberry, 77
  Chenault, 77
Coriander, 150
Coriandrum, 150
Cornus, 79
Cosmos, 19
  annual, 19
  chocolate, 19
  yellow, 19
Cottonwood, 100
  cottonless, 100
Crabapple, 78

Cranberry, high-bush, 109
Cranberrybush, American, 109
Cranesbill, 52
bloodred, 52
bloody, 52
Crataegus, 86
Crocus, 141
Dutch, 141
Cup-and-Saucer vine, 131
Cypress, Siberian, 103
Daffodil, 142
Dahlberg daisy, 20
Dahlia, 143
Daisy, African, 28
Daisy, Cape, 28
Daisy, Dahlberg, 20
Daisy, gloriosa, 13
Dead nettle, 58
spotted, 58
Dill, 151
Dimorphotheca, 28
Dogwood, 79
Dropwort, 61
Dusty Miller, 21
Echinacea, 48
Elderberry, 80
American, 80
black, 80
European, 80
European red, 80
Elm, 81
American, 81
hybrid, 81
English marigold, 15
Eulalia, 164
Euonymus, 82
winged, 82
wintercreeper, 82
Eupatorium, 56
Euphorbia, 49
Exotic love, 135

Fagus, 72
Fall garden mum, 47
False cypress, 83
Fern, cinnamon, 160
Fern, northern maidenhair, 163
Fern, royal, 160
Fescue, blue sheep, 158
Festuca, 158
Fiddlehead fern, 165
Filipendula, 61
Fir, 84
alpine, 84
balsam, 84
Korean, 84
subalpine, 84
white, 84
Firecracker vine, 135
Flame grass, 164
Floss flower, 11
Flowering fern, 160
Flowering onion, 144
Foam flower, 50
Fountain grass, 161
annual, 161
dwarf perennial, 161
red annual, 161
Fringe tree, 85
Chinese, 85
white, 85
Galium, 169
Gayfeather, 59
Kansas, 59
rough, 59
spike, 59
Geranium, 52
cranesbill, 52
ivy-leaved, 22
scented, 22

zonal, 22
Gladiolus, 145
Goat's beard, 51
common, 51
dwarf Korean, 51
giant, 51
Golden fleece, 20
Grape, 132
Groundsel, golden, 60
Gymnocladus, 91
Hamamelis, 112
Hansa, 117
Hardy geranium, 52
Hawthorn, 86
dotted, 86
English, 86
glossy, 86
Russian, 86
Heliopsis, 63
Heliotrope, 23
Heliotropium, 23
Hemlock, ground, 113
Henry Hudson, 118
Heuchera, 53
Honeysuckle (shrub), 87
European fly, 87
Tatarian, 87
winter, 87
Honeysuckle (vine), 133
Brown's, 133
coral, 133
goldflame, 133
hairy, 133
scarlet trumpet, 133
trumpet, 133
yellow, 133
Hope for humanity, 119
Horsechestnut, 88
common, 88

red, 88
Hosta, 54
Hydrangea (shrub), 89
bigleaf, 89
panicle, 89
Peegee, 89
smooth, 89
Hydrangea (vine), 130
Hypoestes, 31
Impatiens, 24
balsam, 24
New Guinea, 24
Indian currant, 77
Ipomoea (foliage), 168
Ipomoea (vine), 135
Iris, 55
Japanese, 55
Siberian, 55
Japanese creeper, 139
Japanese silver grass, 164
Japanese Spurge, 166
Joe-Pye weed, 56
sweet, 56
John Franklin, 120
Johnny-jump-up, 36
Juneberry, 104
Juniper, 90
Chinese, 90
common, 90
creeping, 90
Japanese garden, 90
Rocky Mountain, 90
savin, 90
singleseed, 90
Juniperus, 90
Kentucky coffee tree, 91

Kiwi, 134
 hardy, 134
Kiwi vine,
 variegated, 134
Lady's mantle, 57
 common, 57
Lamium, 58
Lantana, 25
Large fountain, 164
Lathyrus, 137
Lavatera, 26
 tree mallow, 26
Liatris, 59
Ligularia, 60
 bigleaf, 60
 narrow-spiked, 60
 Shevalski's, 60
Lilac, 92
 common, 92
 early-flowering,
 92
 French, 92
 hyacinth-
 flowered, 92
 Japanese tree, 92
 Manchurian, 92
 Meyer, 92
 Preston hybrid, 92
Lilium, 146
Lily, 146
 oriental, 146
 plantain, 54
Linden, 93
 American, 93
 bigleaf, 93
 littleleaf, 93
 Mongolian, 93
 silver, 93
Lobularia, 34
Lonicera (shrub),
 87
Lonicera (vine),
 133
Lungwort, 162
 common, 162
 long-leaved, 162
Macy's Pride, 121

Magnolia, 94
 hybrid, 94
 star, 94
Maiden grass, 164
 variegated, 164
Maidenhair fern,
 163
Malus, 78
Maple, 95
 amur, 95
 hedge, 95
 Korean, 95
 paperbark, 95
 purplebloom, 95
 striped, 95
 Tatarian, 95
Marigold, 27
 African, 27
 American, 27
 Aztec, 27
 English, 15
 French, 27
 pot, 15
 signet, 27
 triploid, 27
Marjoram, 153
Martin Frobisher,
 122
Matteuccia, 165
Meadowsweet, 61
Mentha, 152
Microbiota, 103
Millet, purple
 ornamental, 161
Mina lobata, 135
Mint, 152
 orange mint, 152
 peppermint, 152
 spearmint, 152
Miscanthus, 164
Moonflower, 135
Moosewood, 95
Morden Fireglow,
 123
Morden Snow-
 beauty, 124

Morden Sunrise,
 125
Morning glory, 135
 common, 135
Moss pinks, 65
Mountain ash, 96
 American, 96
 European, 96
 Korean, 96
 showy, 96
Narcissus, 142
Ninebark, 97
 common, 97
 dwarf, 97
Oak, 98
 bur, 98
 mossycup, 98
 swamp white, 98
 white, 98
Obedient plant, 62
Ocimum, 148
Onion, 144
 blue globe, 144
 giant, 144
 nodding, 144
 wild, 144
Orange mint, 152
Oregano, 153
 Greek, 153
Origanum, 153
Osmunda, 160
Osteospermum, 28
Ostrich fern, 165
Ox-eye, 63
Pachysandra, 166
 Allegheny, 166
Paeonia, 64
Painted-tongue, 29
Panicum, 170
Pansy, 36
Parsley, 154
Parthinocissus, 139
Passiflora, 136
Passion flower, 136
 blue, 136
Pelargonium, 22
 scented, 22

Pennisetum, 161
Peony, 64
Peppermint, 152
Perovskia, 66
Petroselinium, 154
Petunia, 30
Phlox, 65
 creeping, 65
 early, 65
 garden, 65
 moss, 65
Physocarpus, 97
Physostegia, 62
Picea, 106
Pine, 99
 Austrian, 99
Pinks, moss, 65
Pinus, 99
Platycodon, 42
Plum, 75
Polka dot plant, 31
Poplar, 100
Poplar, Lombardy,
 100
Populus, 100
Porcupine grass,
 164
Pot marigold, 15
Prunus, 75
Pulmonaria, 162
Queen-of-the-
 meadow, 61
Queen-of-the-
 prairie, 61
Quercus, 98
Red-leafed Rose,
 126
Redbud, 101
 eastern, 101
Redcedar, eastern,
 90
Reed grass, 167
 Foerster's
 feather, 167
Rhododendron, 102
Rhus, 107
Rosa glauca, 126

Rosemary, 155
Rosmarinus, 155
Rudbeckia (annual), 13
Rudbeckia (perennial), 43
Russian cypress, 103
Russian sage, 66
Sage (annual), 32
blue, 32
mealy cup, 32
scarlet, 32
Sage (perennial), 39
silver, 39
white, 39
Sage (herb), 156
Sage, Bethlehem, 162
Salix, 111
Salpiglossis, 29
Salvia (annual), 32
Salvia (herb), 156
Sambucus, 80
Saskatoon, 104
Sedum, 67
autumn joy, 67
Senecio, 21
Serviceberry, 104
Allegheny, 104
apple, 104
downy, 104
Lamarck's, 104
shadblow, 104
Silver vine, 134
Skyflower vine, 128
Snakeroot (*Cimicifuga*), 45
black, 45
Snakeroot (*Eupatorium*), 56
white, 56
Snakeroot (*Lamium*), 59
button, 59
Snapdragon, 33

Snowberry, common, 77
Solenostemon, 18
Sorbus, 96
Spearmint, 152
Speedwell, 68
prostrate, 68
spike, 68
Spider flower, 17
Spiraea, 105
Spirea, 105
bridal wreath, 105
Japanese, 105
Vanhoutte, 105
Spirea, false, 41
Spotted dog, 162
Spruce, 106
black, 106
bog, 106
Colorado, 106
Norway, 106
Serbian, 106
white, 106
Allegheny, 166
Spurge, 49
cushion, 49
flowering, 49
tramp's, 49
wild, 49
Spurge, Japanese, 166
Stonecrop, 67
gold moss, 67
showy, 67
two-row, 67
Sumac, 107
flameleaf, 107
fragrant, 107
lemonade, 107
shining, 107
skunkbush, 107
smooth, 107
staghorn, 107
Summersweet clethra, 108
Sunflower, false, 63

Sunflower, orange, 63
Sweet alyssum, 34
Sweet breath of spring, 87
Sweet pea, 137
Sweet pepperbush, 108
Sweet potato vine, 168
Sweet William, wild, 65
Sweet woodruff, 169
Sweetspire, 108
Switch grass, 170
blue, 170
red, 170
Symphoricarpos, 77
Symphyotrichum, 40
Syringa, 92
Tagetes, 27
Taxus, 113
Thoroughwort, 56
Thuja, 70
Thunbergia, 128
Thyme, 157
common, 157
lemon-scented, 157
Thymophylla, 20
Thymus, 157
Tiarella, 50
Tilia, 93
Trumpet creeper, 138
Trumpet vine, 138
Tulipa, 147
Tulips, 147
Ulmus, 81
Velvet flower, 29
Verbena, 35
garden, 35
shrub, 25

Veronica, 68
Viburnum, 109
Viola, 36
Violet, 36
horned, 36
Virgin's bower, 129
Virginia creeper, 139
Vitis, 132
Weigela, 110
White cedar, eastern, 70
Willow, 111
basket, 111
dappled, 111
Japanese dappled, 111
purple, 111
purple osier, 111
Witchhazel, 112
common, 112
vernal, 112
Woodbine, 139
Woolflower, 16
Wormwood, 39
Yarrow, 69
common, 69
Yew, 113
American, 113
Canadian, 113
English Japanese, 113
Japanese, 113
Zinnia, 37
Mexican, 37

Author Biographies

Don Engebretson is a University of Minnesota Master Gardener and award-winning garden writer who has been featured on HGTV and PBS TV's *Hometime* program. Known as the Renegade Gardener, he is the monthly garden columnist for *Mpls. St. Paul* magazine, a field editor for *Better Homes and Gardens* and a contributor to a variety of gardening magazines. Don is a four-time Garden Globe award winner for excellence in garden feature writing.

Veteran garden writer **Don Williamson** is the co-author of several popular gardening guides. He has a degree in horticultural technology and extensive experience in the design and construction of annual and perennial beds in formal landscape settings.

Author Acknowledgments

It's been a pleasure to have co-authored Lone Pine's series of books focusing on plants for Minnesota and Wisconsin. I hope the readers of this book and the other books in the series gain as much plant and gardening acumen by reading them as I did in researching and helping write them.

—*Don Engebretson*

I am blessed to work with many wonderful people, including the savvy Renegade Gardener, Don Engebretson, and all the great folks at Lone Pine Publishing. I also thank The Creator.

—*Don Williamson*

We thank the following people and organizations for their valuable time and beautiful images: AgCanada, Allison Penko, Anne Gordon, Bailey Nurseries, Chicagoland Grows Inc., David Cavagnaro, Dawn Loewen, Debra Knapke, Derek Fell, Don Doucette, Duncan Kelbaugh, Erika Flatt, Horticolor, J.C. Bakker & Sons, Janet Davis, Jen Fafard, Joan de Grey, Joy Spurr, Kim O'Leary, Laura Peters, Leila Sidi, Marilynn McAra, Mark Turner, Peter Thompstone, Photos.com, Robert Ritchie, Sandra Bit, Tamara Eder, Tim Matheson, Tim Wood and all those who allowed us to photograph their gardens.